About the Authors

The Raven Brothers were born in the United Kingdom. *Hike, Drive, Stayin' Alive!* is their fifth book. The first published work by the authors, *Living the Linger*, tells the story of a journey of lost love and a search for the truth during a road trip through backcountry USA. A year later, the brothers became established travel writers following a life-altering drive from the UK to Vladivostok in a rusty Ford Sierra. Noted by Lonely Planet for their talent to portray an "accurate view of what to expect", the book *Driving the Trans-Siberian* spurred a life on the road. *Carnival Express* was the concluding title in the 'Linger Series' trilogy, and follows two struggling writers on a South America adventure. A period of photojournalism, documenting new and off the beaten track destinations, tribal India, China's deep south and Crimea, led to the release of *Black Sea Circuit*. Seizing a narrow window of opportunity to cross the notorious Caucasus frontier, the book explores great legends from Jason and the Argonauts to a tribe of fierce female warriors known as the Amazons. The release of *Hike, Drive, Stayin' Alive!* signals a return to the duo writing "buttock clenching" travel comedy, with the first in a collection of ten candid stories of adventure by The Raven Brothers.

Also by The Raven Brothers

Living the Linger

Driving the Trans-Siberian

Carnival Express

Black Sea Circuit

Hike, Drive,
Stayin' Alive!

THE RAVEN BROTHERS

samosir
BOOKS

Published by Samosir Books 2020

First published in Great Britain in 2020 by Samosir Books

A CIP catalogue record for this book is available from the British Library

ISBN 9780954884291

To the warmhearted

"Viva la Vida" (Live Life)
Frida Kahlo, 1954

Contents

Wellness in Berlin

Exit Warschauer Strasse station at midnight and the sound of punk and techno erupts from air vents beneath your feet. Cross the two tiered Brick Gothic Oberbaum Bridge, from the former east of Berlin to the west, and the thunder of the metro and an energy fuelled by buskers and beggars is invigorating. My first trip to Berlin started out as three days and ended up lasting six months. I left the city aboard a flight to London with an enormous grin across my face and a hangover that delayed my return. One year later, the invitation to look after an apartment for a friend lured me back. I had recently finished co-writing a book about the Black Sea with Chris, and it seemed like the perfect opportunity to re-visit and maybe write about a destination I knew fairly well. Searching for inspiration, I stumbled across an exhibition celebrating a period in time when David Bowie lived in Berlin. At the age of thirty, the already successful musician left Los Angeles and moved to Germany in a bid to escape drug addiction and improve his wellbeing. He shared an apartment with Iggy Pop and recorded three albums between 1977 and 1979. It suddenly occurred to me that if two of the biggest wreckheads known to rock 'n' roll could find sanctuary in Berlin, maybe so could I.

Weaving between the sandstone columns of the Brandenburg Gate, I approach the grand entrance of the Hotel Adlon. I'm met by Sabina, the Director of PR, beneath a spectacular glass dome roof.

'The Queen of the United Kingdom and Prince Phillip stayed here only a few months ago.'

I raise an eyebrow. 'I hope they were well behaved.'

Sabina fights a smile. 'So, you are writing about wellness?'

'Yes, that's the plan.'

'Simon, as you know, Berlin is a party city. However, we also know how to relax. You must experience the sauna infusions at Vabali in Fritz Schloss Park and there are many beautiful Turkish hamams. Of course, we have a wonderful wellness area at the Adlon, which we are looking forward to sharing with you.'

'You also mentioned singing bowl therapy and meditation?'

'That's correct, I have arranged for you to spend an hour with Vijay our resident yoga master and meditation coach. He is one of the best in Berlin.'

* * *

Underdressed and out of place, I slide up to the reception desk of a five star hotel.

'*Hallo, guten tag.* Would you mind pointing me in the direction of your singing bowl department, please? I think it's in the guru lounge area.'

The receptionist drops her smile, and frowns. 'The guru lounge area? Are you sure you are in the right place, sir?'

'This is the Hotel Adlon? My brother is enjoying your

soul nourishing treatments in one of Berlin's most tranquil wellness havens.'

'I think you are referring to the Adlon Spa by Resense?' she smiles. 'Ride the elevator one floor down.'

Ambient lighting illuminates a marble vault beneath the streets of Berlin. I'm invited to sit on a comfortable leather sofa. A spa assistant serves me an exotic fruit drink with a jungle of green foliage growing out of the top. I am about to take a sip when I hear three loud bangs from a gong. The door to a nearby treatment room swings open and my brother Simon appears wearing black harem trousers and a collarless tunic.

I leap to my feet. 'Buddy, made it back to Berlin!'

Si looks surprised, almost annoyed to see me.

'How did you know I was here?' he snaps, self-consciously drawing his hair back in a ponytail.

'You sent me a voice message.'

'Did I?'

'Yes, you said, "Chris, going to get bing-bang-bonged by singing bowls at the Adlon Saturday afternoon. Freebie. See ya next week."'

His eyes widen. 'Look, I'm right in the middle of therapy. I need to wrap things up with Vijay. Just sit back down and don't touch anything!'

Exiting the hotel, we jump on a metro train. Si looks more stressed than usual.

'You absolute buffoon!' he cries. 'You completely embarrassed me.'

'It wasn't that bad. Besides, it was fairly obvious you were on the blag.'

'How dare you. Ok, so maybe my article for a leading London newspaper fell through, but I'll write about my experience at the Adlon. They'll get coverage one way or another, you'll see.'

'What were you doing there, anyway?'

Si looks reflective. 'I wanted to try something different. If we carry on at the rate we're going we'll be six feet under in a decade.'

'You're not having a midlife crisis, are you?'

'Of course not. Vijay is a health master, the best in Berlin. Singing bowl therapy is an ancient healing practice that has the power to address physical and psychological concerns through the use of sound. He used the bowls to pass vibrations through my body revealing problems with digestion, emotions, health issues and mental wellbeing.'

'And what did he find?'

'Nothing.'

I burst out laughing. 'Good job it was free.'

'Psychologically, I think he may have awoken something. It's like Vijay was saying, many religions and cultures use sound to some extent. Church bells of Christianity, the Islamic call to prayer, chanting and mantras in Buddhism, Sikhism and Hinduism.'

'Careful Si, don't get brainwashed and become a Harry Krishna.'

'It's Hare Krishna. Anyway, you don't have to worry. It's very unlikely I'll be joining a cult anytime soon.'

'That's good news, but what did he awaken?'

'Are you taking the piss?'

'No, I'm only curious.'

'Ok, well, after the singing bowl treatment was over, I found myself sharing with Vijay my innermost frustrations. You have to understand, Chris, for the first time in my life I'm beginning to feel a strong desire to change course.'

'I told you it was a midlife crisis.'

The metro screeches into Alexanderplatz and the doors burst open.

'Laugh all you like, buddy, but watch this space. Things are about to change around here. In fact, I recommend you buckle up and come along for the ride. Hedonism to health, let's jump through these metro doors and embark on a path of wellness.'

The urgent sound of an alarm wakes me with a start. I fumble for my phone and knock over a bottle of beer onto the wooden floorboards. Stripped to his underpants, Si is hanging half off the adjacent couch. My surprise visit yesterday afternoon had led to us drinking a few too many Erdingers in a lively bar in Kreuzberg. Determined not to break his routine of fitness, Si drags his aging bones off the couch and attempts a short run around the block. He returns twenty minutes later struggling for breath.

'This is great!' I smile, watching with intrigue, as the female yoga instructor on the TV contorts her body into a position known as the downward facing dog.

Si rolls his eyes. 'You're supposed to practise yoga not watch it. How long are you staying?'

'Oh, that's charming. You're already asking when I'm leaving. I've been on a long and treacherous journey to get here.'

'It was a two hour flight.'

'Listen, you don't have to worry. I'm going to eat my bratwurst, finish my coffee and rock over to Hamburg.'

'Hamburg?'

'I've got a date with a plane.'

'Where are you jetting off to?'

'I'm not flying anywhere. It's a press tour of the Airbus assembly factory. I've been invited to watch skilled engineers screwing on the wings. I'll be back in a few days.'

'Plane geek.'

'Aviation enthusiast if you don't mind.'

'I'm meeting Marlene, my fitness coach this afternoon.'

I fight a smile. 'Be careful you don't snap in half.'

'Chris, aren't you even a little bit concerned about your health? I mean, you've put on a lot of chunk in recent months.'

'Hey, I'm big boned.'

Si points a warning finger. 'Well, something's got to give!'

* * *

Keen to set the wellness wheels in motion before I become distracted, or change my mind, I boot Chris out of the apartment and head across town. I meet Marlene at a riverside cafe close to her yoga studio. She entertains me with stories of her experience living in London during the late eighties. Marlene worked as a property agent when the city was rammed full of smoky pubs, and the concept of exercise was reserved mainly for professional athletes, soldiers or prisoners serving time.

'All I could find were damp and musty sports halls with iron weights and medicine balls,' Marlene smiles. 'The concept of the modern health club had yet to arrive.'

Marlene's first job was working in a Farringdon pub close to Smithfield meat market. Her shift started at 6am, and she recalls men wearing blood-soaked overalls drinking pints of beer for breakfast. She later worked in the City. The concept of the "liquid lunch" was a cultural pasttime. It was Madonna and Sting who inspired her to get into yoga. She learnt the basics at home from yoga workout videos and books. Immediately she was addicted. Quitting her job, she travelled the world and got married in Vegas before eventually settling in Berlin in 1991. It was an exciting period, because the Wall had only recently fallen and East and West Berlin was slowly becoming one city again. In the years of separation, this area around Kreuzberg was considered home to the Berlin music scene. In the 1970s David Bowie and Iggy Pop regularly played at the SO36 club, which was well-known at the time as a new wave venue. Reunification had doubled the size of Berlin overnight. With a liberal attitude to expression and cheap rent, the city developed a reputation for being tolerant towards cultural integration and rapidly grew into an epicentre of hedonism and one of the hippest city destinations in Europe. Marlene became a certified YogaVeda teacher and Ayurveda therapist, and by pure coincidence worked for many years at the Hotel Adlon. I ask Marlene if she thinks I have a chance of finding wellness in Berlin.

She glances down at my glass of frothy Weiss bier and laughs hysterically. 'Sure, why not. No one condition is permanent.'

Sweeping by Marlene's yoga studio, we collect bicycles and pedal through the leafy green streets. I haven't ridden a bike for a while, but I soon find my rhythm and smile into a gentle summer breeze. With Marlene leading the way, we cycle through Görlitzer Park to Schlesisches Tor and soon arrive at Treptower Park. We ditch the bicycles and sprint up the steps of an enormous Soviet War Memorial. Marlene performs a victory dance in the style of Rocky. Out of breath, I look up at the imposing statue of a soldier who is clutching a child and wielding a sword. At his feet is a broken swastika.

'You are seriously out of shape, Simon,' observes Marlene. 'I regularly run here with my partner.'

'I followed your advice and started training last week, but it's taking time to get fit.'

'What about yoga?'

'Yes, yoga, too. The video you sent me is brilliant. I've never felt more energised and clearer in my mind.'

'I'm pleased it's working for you. In my opinion, it would be hugely beneficial if yoga were encouraged from a young age. We forget to stretch and breathe and take a brief moment each day to reboot the brain.'

A party of overexcited school kids take selfies on the steps before being frantically herded away by their stressed supervisor.

'I want to show you something,' Marlene smiles. 'Stand tall with your feet apart and your hands on your hips.'

'Do I have to?'

'Yes, I want to teach you how to perform the Wonder Woman.'

'The Wonder Woman?'

Marlene grabs my arms and physically forces me into position.

'Straighten your posture and close your eyes. Focus on your breathing. Ok, now inhale through your mouth and exhale out of your nose. Fill your lungs and your chest with oxygen. Push out the air with your abdomen. Do this twenty times.'

With my hands on my hips, I obediently follow Marlene's request. By the time I reach the last breath, I feel a noticeable increase in my energy levels, which I assume is associated with the intake of oxygen into my bloodstream. When I open my eyes, I look around and find Marlene is nowhere to be seen. An old chap squeezes past on the top step of the monument and casts me a look of concern. I spot Marlene laughing over by our bicycles.

We pedal to a large lake and spend the remainder of the afternoon in a rowing boat. Propelling the vessel forward with heavy wooden oars, Marlene sunbathes at the bow while I sweat in the heat.

'All the way around the island?' I gasp, squinting in the bright sunlight.

'Twice,' Marlene replies, slipping on a floppy sun hat and shades.

'I'm seriously beginning to dislike exercise.'

'Once you are physically fit you will find a rhythm to your daily health regime. Besides, it's fun watching you work.'

I take a moment to appreciate my beautiful surroundings, a pair of white swans glide past.

'Who are your yoga clients?' I ask.

'Mainly business professionals. There are many new startups in Berlin. They understand the benefits of investing in the health and wellbeing of their employees.'

'Do you also teach them to stand in the Wonder Woman pose?'

'Absolutely,' she laughs. 'According to Harvard research, standing in a power pose dramatically raises testosterone levels.'

'How is that beneficial?'

'It helps with confidence. The position also decreases cortisol levels. Less cortisol in the body equals lower stress levels.'

'That's incredible, so standing tall for a few minutes can give you a natural chemical advantage.'

'Of course,' she nods. 'Imagine how useful it can be to temporarily boost your confidence levels before an important business meeting, a public speaking event or an exam.'

'Certainly healthier than a cigarette, a stiff drink or a line of cocaine.'

Marlene smiles. 'Exactly. You have so much potential Simon, but look at the way you sit. You are a typical hunched over writer. It's hardly surprising you haven't got the energy to exercise. What an awful way to start your day. Now straighten your back, seize those oars and row!'

Up with the birds, I sprint through one of the largest urban gardens in Germany. Occupying 520 acres of prime real estate, the Tiergarten is the green heart of Berlin that stretches west from the Brandenburg Gate in a maze of walking trails and cycle paths. I narrowly avoid being mowed down by a speeding bicycle, and continue to run alongside the arrow straight Landwehr canal. I pass enormous aviaries at the rear of Berlin zoo, housing colourful exotic water birds. I pause to catch my breath in front of an enclosure containing South American llamas. Inhaling the sweet smell of animal dung, I hear the sound of a lion roar in the distance. My phone begins to buzz. It's Chris.

'Hey, buddy, how's Hamburg?'

'Guess where I am?'

'Drinking beer on the Reeperbahn?'

'Nope, I'm on the beach!'

'I thought Hamburg was inland?'

'You're forgetting the Elbe. Huge container ships keep gliding past.'

'What time does your plane geek tour start?'

'One o'clock. Just enough time for a swim.'

'In the river?'

'It's only partially toxic. Did you snap in half yesterday?'

'No, survived it. Marlene is a hard taskmaster. Although, it could happen in half an hour, I'm about to attempt Tai Chi.'

'Tai Chi?'

'It's similar to Wing Chun.'

'Is that a Chinese soup?'

'You're joking, right?'

'Oooh, the water's freeezing!' Chris howls. 'Time to say hello to the fishes. See you tomorrow, kiddo.'

The line cuts dead.

I arrive at the Shaolin Tempel Deutschland, and look with intrigue at two large concrete dragons that guard the entrance to the modern red and yellow building with picture windows. Yusuf, a medical doctor who regularly visits the temple, meets me outside. He is dressed in black and carrying what appears to be a sword over his shoulder. I am introduced to the administrator of the temple, the abbot, Grand Master Shi Yong Chuan. Wearing mustard robes, the monk respectfully bows her shaven head and invites me to join the morning Tai Chi class. Participating in the hour long session, I attempt to mirror the instructor's moves. It is faster than I had expected, and I struggle to keep my balance and stumble on more than one occasion. The monk separates me from the group and demonstrates a routine that I must repeat, whilst the core of the class perform an exercise with fake swords. At the front of the room there is a large gold statue of Buddha, which watches over us. Yusuf looks deep in concentration and cuts the air with expert precision that defies his years.

Following the group to a windowless room on the ground floor, I experience a second half hour session of Qi Gong with Shi Yong Chuan. She sits cross-legged infront of the class, mimicking the statue of Buddha. Following a routine, which bizarrely involves slapping our cheeks and swilling spit around the inside of our mouths, we rub the palms of our hands quickly together and transfer the heat generated by friction to our faces, eyes, ears, feet, arms and knees. Despite the faint sound of drilling and hammering from a nearby construction site, I feel safe inside the temple walls and calm in the presence of the monk. Afterwards we chant sounds in unison. The powerful energy this creates is surprising, and I leave the centre feeling completely enthralled by the experience.

Yusuf seems pleased I enjoyed my introductory class and invites me for sushi. Devouring a basket of steamed fish and vegetables, Yusuf reveals that although the Grand Master may appear passive, she is in fact highly skilled in Kung Fu and Tai Chi and has won endless trophies at martial arts tournaments. He explains that the exercise I was taught was Yang Style 16 Form. Each movement in the sequence has a name. Yusuf begins to demonstrate each move.

'Commencing form,' he smiles raising his arms. 'Part the wild horse's mane, white crane spreads its wings, brush knee, deflect, parry and punch.'

'Ah, ok, I see now. That would certainly help me to remember all sixteen moves.'

'Yes, it is like a dance. Repulse the monkey, maiden works her shuttle, needle at the bottom of the sea and flash arms like a fan.'

I always thought Tai Chi was passive and slow, and it is interesting to discover that Shaolin style Tai Chi is a lot faster. They wear black almost like Kung Fu and it shares similarities with Chen style from China's Hunan Province. I make a joke about Qi Gong being lethal. Yusuf fails to look amused. I learn that the word "qi" or (chi) literally means "life energy", and that Qi Gong is used in the cultivation and balance of this energy through coordinated body posture and movement, meditation and breathing.

'Qi gong can help awaken your true nature and develop your human potential,' Yusuf adds. 'It is a very powerful skill.'

Yusuf finds Tai Chi and Qi Gong keep him fit and healthy and his mind focused, and they have dramatically improved his posture and confidence. In his work as a doctor in a hospital he regularly sees patients, particularly in their twilight years, with injuries related to poor physical health, bad backs, hips, knees, stiff necks and dislocated shoulders. He believes many of these issues can be prevented with increased muscle strength and mobility. Buddhist ceremonies are held regularly in the Shaolin Temple, and they pray regularly for peace, wellbeing and health. I ask Yusuf if he is a Buddhist and he smiles and explains that belief is not necessary for participation at the Shaolin Temple. He identifies closely with the Buddhist philosophy, and finds having the temple in his life hugely beneficial. Contemplating the idea of shaving my head and becoming a monk, I thank Yusuf for his kind introduction to the world of Buddhist martial arts and leave the restaurant powered by protein and green tea.

Following an afternoon of eye opening relaxation at Vabali Spa, I exit into the street clean as a whistle and ready for an early night. The newly built wellness retreat that my PR contact Roaya had accurately described as, "a garden oasis in the heart of Berlin" had been an experience of luxury pampering beyond my wildest imagination. Water pools, Ayurvedic massages and endless sauna infusions, that were so hot, at one stage I feared my eyeballs might burst into flames. Rubbing crushed ice all over my naked body in an atmospherically lit sauna garden, following a particularly memorable eucalyptus cleansing steam bath, is an experience I am unlikely to ever forget. I walk down to the Spree and follow the river to Friedrichstrasse. It feels like the last day of summer. I spot patches of orange leaves in the trees as autumn eagerly approaches. A cyclist speeds past and I'm reminded of my cycle adventure with Marlene. Spying Norman Foster's iconic glass dome atop the Reichstag parliament building, I smile at the memory of my experience with Sabina and Vijay at the nearby Adlon. A thought suddenly darts into my mind. Have I finally left my extended youth behind? Have my rock 'n' roll years seriously been replaced by menthol scented infusions, yoga and Tai Chi? I turn to David Bowie, and wonder what advice the Thin White Duke might offer to assist me during this transitional phase of my life. But then I remember he is dead. He died from liver cancer in his New York City apartment aged 69. According to his will, he requested for his ashes to be scattered in Indonesia in accordance with the Buddhist rituals of Bali. Death is of course unpredictable, who knows when our time may arrive, and maybe Bowie's drug addiction in the 1970s was completely unrelated to his heart attack in 2004 and relatively premature death. Bowie was a rich man. If his millions could not save him, what chance did an average Joe like me or Chris have if illness were to strike? When I was a young rock 'n' roller, I had the attitude live fast, die young. The risk of adventure travel had prolonged this neglect of my health, using it as an excuse for living roughly, as I felt I might perish anyway on the next death road. But I have not died yet. I have reached middle age. Still enjoying the thrill aboard the colourful carousel of life, I am fairly sure I am not yet ready to get off. I want the ride to last as long as possible, at least until I have white hair. It seems clear to me now that we have reached tipping point. If we fail to invest in our health all of the thrills of adventure that we have survived could result in being the cause of our demise. So travel might still kill us, but far worse would be for the adventures to cause illness through disregard of our wellbeing.

* * *

Standing in the dark outside Si's apartment building, I press the buzzer to the intercom. I clomp up the wooden staircase to the fourth floor. The lock snaps open, and he peers around the door.

'The Späti on the corner is open twenty-four hours a day. Berlin rocks!'

Si narrows his eyes. 'It's five o'clock in the morning.'

'Party hour!'

I follow my brother into the kitchen. He plonks himself down at the table. 'How was Hamburg?'

'Amazing! Those Hanseatic folk certainly know how to live.'

I begin to unscrew the lid off a bottle of wine.

Si shakes his head in despair. 'Hanging out with you is going to kill me.'

'What are you talking about? Surely one glass of wine is good for you.'

Si takes a moment to muse over my words. He blinks madly in a moment of clarity and rises to his feet. 'Hey, do you know what, I think you could be onto something there.'

'Finally! We don't have to completely cut the fun. A healthy balance is all about moderation, dear boy.'

Joining me in a five a.m. glass of German juice, Si's mood appears to dramatically improve. We begin brainstorming trip ideas.

'Norway,' I wink. 'It's an adventure playground.'

'Norway? Do you realise how much a Frappuccino costs in that country?'

'Forget about the budget of the trip. Let's drive to

Nordkapp! It's the northernmost point of Europe. Think open highways, fjords and cute reindeer. We can catch fish and forage for wild food, build campfires and grow big beards like Viking warriors or mountain men.'

Si takes a sip of wine and screws up his face. 'Is this cooking wine?'

'Our very last glass,' I laugh, raising a toast.

The cheap and nasty wine kick starts our day with a bang. Si leaps into action and prepares a healthy breakfast of champions, nectarine, pineapple, red grapefruit and honeydew melon with creamy yoghurt, followed by thin strips of smoked salmon on lightly toasted German rye bread with cherry tomatoes and goat's cheese. We call a few friends and arrange a get together. Si suggests we walk the 5km to Mauer Park instead of catching the tram. I massage my swollen stomach as we wander through the sunny streets.

Sunday in Mauer Park is undoubtedly one of the more unique gatherings in Berlin, where artisans meet to sell art, jewellery, upcycled furniture, old vinyl, vintage cameras, bicycles, secondhand clothes, household inventions and rusty musical instruments. Organic coffee, vegan ice cream, craft beer and sizzling food trucks compete side by side to feed the hungry masses. We snake across the park where funky hipsters hula hoop, juggle and write poems on typewriters. Graffiti artists on a hilltop work their magic on walls overlooking the city, and brave performers belt out karaoke classics on the impromptu stage in front of a packed crowd. We laze on the grass and observe the spectacle of Berlin all around us. Nearby, a busker plays psychedelic didgeridoo, while a group of Spanish acrobats take turns walking a tightrope strung between two trees. Soaking up the rays with good people, Si's psychologist friend, Afra, reveals that relaxation, meditation and good sleep is the ultimate wellness treatment that is completely free and often ignored. As daylight fades, a reggae band powers into action. Smoke from charcoal barbecues drifts around our feet. We are drawn into the crowd. The striking guy singing shakes his dreads with captivating rhythm, "Sun beneath the reef," he growls into the microphone. "Music in your heart!".

A Little Hike to the Top of the World

'A penguin and a polar bear have never met?'

My eyes narrow as I suck on a heavily salted chunk of salmiak liquorice, a popular Nordic confectionery. 'Not in the wild. Polar bears live in the northern hemisphere, penguins in the south. They're poles apart.'

Si launches a paper aeroplane at the window screen. 'It would be just our luck to be savaged to death out here. Heads torn from our torsos, arms legs and innards scattered across the virgin white snow.'

I crack a smile. 'Unlikely to happen. The nearest polar bears are still seven-hundred and fifty kilometres north of Nordkapp on the remote island of Svalbard.'

I pull up my collars and look out into the mist. If by some freak chance a rogue bear did happen to swim to mainland Europe, all we have to protect ourselves is a broken golf umbrella. According to survival experts, if attacked, the best course of action is to act like a threat. I turn to Si, who madly shakes his long hair and drums a tune on the dashboard.

Mission

Travel by car from the remote Lofoten archipelago to the North Cape, and hike the Knivskjellodden trail to the extreme northernmost point of Europe.

Destination

Norway. A country in Scandinavia famed for its natural beauty, fjords, the midnight sun, oil, the cheese slicer, reindeer, Sami people, the aurora, cod, the paper clip, Nobel Peace Prize, Vikings, trolls, Edvard Munch expressionist painter (The Scream), lefse (traditional flatbread), and a-ha (popular Norwegian band from the 80s).

Vehicle

Vauxhall (Opel) Corsa 1.0 litre hatchback. Disadvantages: It is very small. Advantages: Good on fuel.

Arctic Experience

Built an igloo in the garden when we were seven years old.

Risk factor

Medium/high: Drive into a fjord, trip over a rock, stray off the trail, fall off a cliff or get eaten by a reindeer.

* * *

1 week ago...

In the bustling harbour village of Å, we look in wonder at a dolphin-size halibut hung by its tail from a mini crane. Chris drops to one knee and fires off a shot with his Nikon of the bizarre looking fish, which appears to interrogate us with its beady eyes. Below a row of red wooden rorbuer fisherman's houses, freshly caught cod is loaded onto the quayside from a motorboat. The echoing cry of seagulls can be heard all around us as they swoop low overhead. We are roughly 150km north of the Arctic Circle, at the furthest point south of the Lofoten archipelago; a chain of islands pointing west towards Iceland like a crooked finger.

Squeezing behind the wheel of our little car, Chris fashions three weeks beard growth, but looks more hobo than Soho. My wild, out of control hair blows vigorously in the wind, as me make our way through a prehistoric world of granite cliffs that plunge into the Norwegian Sea. Cormorants, puffins, otters and seals thrive in endless bays, while the deep ocean attracts sperm whales and giant squid weighing up to a ton. We begin to see wooden cod drying racks called *hjell* at the roadside. They await the arrival of Norwegian Arctic cod from the Barents Sea that spawn here in the Lofoten's warm waters in the middle of winter. Preserving fish naturally in the sun and salty sea air is a thousand year old tradition, which enabled Viking warriors to transport fish enormous distances by boat. It also provided them with a constant food supply during seafaring raids of the British Isles in the late 8th century. The first recorded Viking raid on England was in 789 AD, when a group of Norsemen landed on the Isle of Portland in Dorset. By the 11th century, Viking trade, exploration and influence spanned from Turkey to North America. Not all Norsemen and women were brutal savage warriors who drank out of skulls. History naturally leans towards the dramatic. In reality, the majority of people lived peaceful lives as fisherfolk, skilled woodmen, storytellers, poets, and farmers that raised cattle and grew barley, oats and rye.

* * *

Delivered through the jagged mountains via numerous tunnels, we leapfrog between islands towards the mainland and arrive in the bustling harbour town of Svolvær. Cafe's and souvenir shops compete for space next to upmarket art galleries and luxury boutiques. In the window of a bookstore, an antique leather bound book is open at a page with a beautiful illustration of a whale. It is the story of *Moby Dick* by Herman Melville.

Si reads aloud. '"Aye, my hearties all round; it was Moby Dick that dismasted me; Moby Dick that brought me to this dead stump I stand on now. Aye, aye," he shouted with a terrific, loud, animal sob, like that of a heart-stricken moose. "Aye, aye! I'll chase him round Good Hope, and round the Horn, and round the Norway Maelstrom."' Si frowns. 'Where's the Norway Maelstrom?'

'They are massive whirlpools in the sea off the coast of the Lofoten Islands near to the village of Å. The biggest is fifty metres in diameter, ripples a metre high. You get caught up in that, you're fish food.' I take a bite out of a slice of kvæfjordkake (sponge cake baked with meringue, vanilla cream and almonds).

'Don't you ever stop eating?'

'Food is energy, hippie boy. All of this sea air is making me hungry.'

From out of nowhere a harlequin Great Dane appears. I

freeze on the spot as it sniffs the cake in my hand. A guy with white hair slides up beside me. He is incredibly tall and has an uncanny likeness to the fashion designer Karl Lagerfeld, minus the makeup and pout.

'He only gets annoyed if you try to ride him like a horse,' he warns, smiling through clenched teeth. 'Where are you from?'

I strike my explorer pose. 'England. We are on a perilous journey to reach the North Cape.'

Si rolls his eyes. 'This is a lively little town.'

'Ja, always in the tourist season. The winter is very different. For three months the sun it does not rise.' He releases an astonishingly deep sigh. 'I do not go out of the house so much at this time.'

With mountains as a backdrop, Svolvær's natural harbour is a hive of activity. Tour boats offer whale and dolphin safaris, and seafarers of all ages relax aboard yachts and sailing boats. A passenger ferry returning from the neighbouring islands of Skrova enters the harbour and glides slowly up to the jetty.

'So many fishing boats here,' Si observes.

Isak disagrees. 'These days, not so much. When my grandfather first came here in the nineteen-forties there were twenty thousand people living in Svolvær. Today, only four thousand.'

'Because there are less fish?'

'No, no, this is not the reason. Big trawlers and factory ships were introduced. They require less people. Technology will eventually replace us all.'

I point at the illustration of Moby Dick. 'Can you still hunt whales in Norway?'

'Ja, sure. We have a legal quota in Norway. Permit holders can hunt a thousand minke whales every season, but they catch only five-hundred. Whale meat is not a good business anymore. You can find whale steak on the menu in tourist restaurants, but it is overpriced.'

A woman wearing a white roll neck sweater exits the bookstore and fusses over the giant dog. It leaps up and tries to lick her face.

She nods a hello to Isak and turns to us with a smile. 'Welcome to Svolvær. Isn't this place awesome?'

'Beautiful,' I reply. 'Hey, are you from the United States?'

'Why, do I look like a movie star?' she laughs.

'Halle Berry springs to mind.'

'Wow, you're too kind. I'm actually Norwegian, from Oslo, but I did live in New York for five years. I'm totally in love with this town. It's my third summer here. I'm Ella by the way. I'm a seascape artist.'

'I'm a huge fan of Houdini!'

Ella frowns. 'Houdini?'

Si steps forward. 'He's fooling around. You're joking, right?'

'Yes! Yes, of course. You're a seascape artist not an escape artist. Although, that would also be great.'

With Ella's business card tucked safely in the back of my notebook, we bid farewell and spend the afternoon photographing this beautiful town before returning to the car. Si points out Fløya Mountain that looms overhead, with its twin peaks known as the Svolvær Goat. He mumbles something about suicidal adrenalin junkies, who leap between the two horns for kicks. I can see his lips moving, but my mind is elsewhere. In a land of breathtaking scenery and dreamy light, I fantasise about hanging my hat here for a while. Maybe I could grow a big beard, change my name to Odin and live as an artisan by the ocean, at least until the winter arrives.

A deserted highway transports us to the mainland and the port of Narvik. Studying his notes, Chris reveals the fiercest clash since the invasion of Poland erupted here during World War II. The town had become the focus of Nazi Germany, who wanted to seize control of the ice-free harbour in a bid to secure transportation of iron ore from nearby mines in Sweden. We set up camp for the night at a tourist viewpoint overlooking the tranquil Ofotfjorden. Information boards display black and white photographs of war ships and soldiers marching with weapons through blizzards. Scouring the deserted shoreline for firewood, Chris stumbles across a stash of plump mussels. Harvesting the vitamin rich seafood, we build a fire in the shelter of the rocks and watch the flames lick the still air. In a region of Europe where the natural world dwarfs humanity, we sit and absorb the heavenly aromas of shellfish, garlic and onion bubbling away in the saucepan. Over a mug of hot coffee, with a dash of brandy, Chris explains how Vikings would collect a special fungus from trees and urinate on it. The sodium nitrate in the urine enabled the fungus to smoulder for days, giving these canny Viking warriors the power to easily light a fire while on the move.

'Hey, mechanically reclaimed fish carcass is actually quite tasty,' Chris sings, tucking into a pre-dinner snack.

'Better get used to it.'

'Keep your eyes peeled for road kill.'

'I'd rather starve to death than eat a pancake flat rabbit with tyre marks across its face.'

'There must be tons of berries, roots, seeds and edible mushrooms we can feast on out here.'

'You clearly haven't read *Into the Wild*. I think the

answer is to conserve fuel. Petrol is two euros a litre, that's ninety percent of our daily budget. We can coast downhill, ease up on the gas and maybe cut out beer for a week.'

'What? No way, that's completely unacceptable,' Chris laughs. 'We need fuel, too. We won't get far on empty. Maybe we can find another passenger.'

'I'm not sure if you've noticed, but there isn't a single soul for miles around.'

Sat at the top of the world in the land of the midnight sun, we look out across the glistening fjord. Late at night when the sun is at its lowest in the sky, Earth's fireball hovers above the horizon creating a long drawn out sunset. Failing to get dark, we are able to sit outside in comfort at any hour without the need for artificial light. Chris plucks a particularly plump mussel from its shell. He is about to pop it into his mouth, when we both look in a frozen moment of surprise at the sail of a large black submarine approaching low in the water. Leaping to our feet, we watch in stunned silence as the rather intimidating vessel glides past.

'You think it's the Norwegian navy?' Chris beams with excitement.

'It could be the Russians on a spying mission.'

'What's NATO's telephone number?'

'It's 07746...how am I supposed to know!'

Chris waves his arms in the air. 'Hello!' he cries.

I imagine the crew inside the submarine monitoring us on a screen via the periscope, questioning whether they should consider the savages a threat. Identifying a nearby naval station on the map, we watch with fascination as the submarine disappears out of sight. Alone once more, we return to the warmth of the fire and continue our banquet of Norwegian shellfish beneath a vast sky.

Braving the icy, submarine infested waters of the fjord, I join Si for an early morning truckers wash. With patches of snow covering the tops of the surrounding hills, we re-join the E6 highway that has carried us an incredible 2,000km north from the city of Malmö in southern Sweden.

We arrive in Tromsø (Gateway to the Arctic) with Norwegian folk music blasting from the speakers.

'Check out that church,' Si nods, as we roll through the suburbs of the city. 'The design was inspired by the shape of an iceberg or a traditional Lavvu tent.'

'What's a lavvu tent?'

'Similar to a wigwam.'

We cross the Tromsø Bridge that arches across the Tromsøysundet strait to the island of Tromsøyaand. A Hurtigruten Arctic cruise ship is moored in the city port.

Si rolls up his window to block out a fierce crosswind. 'Apparently, this district around Tromsø is located in the middle of the Northern Lights Oval, which means it is one of the best places in the world to witness the polar lights natural phenomenon.'

'The areola?' I wait to see Si's reaction before cracking a smile. 'I've actually got an app on my phone that shows aurora activity in real-time. Unfortunately, it's the wrong time of year to witness the magical light show. You need freezing cold conditions, clear dark night skies and, of course, a powerful geomagnetic storm.'

Heading for the port, Si weaves through the bustling streets of a city that is one of the largest settlements closest to the North Pole. Grinning into an icy breeze, we peer up at a taxidermy polar bear rearing up on its hind legs in front of a harbourside restaurant. It has been made to look menacing. Polar bears can weigh in excess of 700kg and reach three metres in height. It is a grisly reminder of Tromsø's past as a centuries-old trading station that once attracted hunters of polar bears, walruses and seals. Nearby a second stuffed bear has been plonked outside a souvenir shop. A handwritten sign placed on its back instructs people not to sit on it. Soaking up the atmosphere of an Arctic pedestrian shopping street in midsummer, we begin to feel peckish. The price of the food in the many cafes and restaurants is eye-wateringly high, so we agree instead to sit in a park and devour fish cutlet and grilled shrimps in a bun. Si wanders over to a large statue.

'Introducing Mr Roald Amundsen!'

'Who was he?'

'This chap was a famous polar explorer. He set off from right here in Tromsø on his Antarctic expedition.'

'Antarctic?'

'Yep, there was a bit of a race to reach the Poles at the beginning of the last century. When he heard the Americans had claimed to have successfully arrived at the North Pole, he rerouted to Antarctica. Sailed south by ship from Oslo.'

'Penguins instead of polar bears. Wise move.' I take a large bite of ocean in a bun.

'He made it, anyway. First human to reach the South Pole.'

'Is he still alive?'

'Died warm in his bed aged a hundred and three.'

'How lovely.'

'If it were true…sadly, his plane crashed into the Barents Sea. His body was never found.'

'Didn't know when to stop. Adventure is addictive.'

Si nods. 'Complete thrill seeker. In addition to the South Pole, he made the first successful voyage by ship through the Northwest Passage. He wrote in his book *The*

South Pole. "Everything is on a reduced scale here in the Polar regions; we can't afford to be extravagant."'

Cheered on by the piercing sound of a seagull wailing overhead, I beat Si to the wheel and we continue on our very own microscopic version of an Arctic adventure. Considering we are now 600km north of the Arctic Circle, it is surprisingly warm and sunny thanks to the North Atlantic drift. Re-joining the old faithful E6 highway, we cruise along the shoreline of Lyngenfjord. Lyngen lamb and delicious Lyngen shrimps are produced here, and the region even claims to have the world's northernmost whisky distillery. Booze to one side we push closer to Finnmark, the largest county in Norway and the last leg of our journey before we reach our mission to hike the Knivskjellodden trail to the North Cape.

* * *

'Sami country!' I sing, as we skim over the top of a corner of Lapland that on the map looks uncannily like a mitten glove.

'Who exactly are the Sami people?'

'A Finno-Ugric people who inhabit Sapmi.'

Chris frowns. 'Did you just make that up?'

'Nope. Traditionally, the Sami people work as semi-nomadic reindeer herders.'

'Rudolph sausages.'

'Devouring Santa's transport is strictly prohibited, I'm afraid.'

A giant hare suddenly dashes out into the road. Chris swerves sharply in the hope of mowing it down. It escapes by the fluff of its tail and disappears into the forest. He bangs his fist on the steering wheel out of frustration. I make a mental note to invest in any form of protein at the next available opportunity.

Entering the Kvænangsfjellet mountain pass, we trade views over the shimmering waters of Kvænangen fjord with the equally spectacular Oksfjorden. Stumbling across a roadside market in a scenic lay-by, we screech to a halt by a distance marker that reveals we are now only 350km away from Nordkapp. We browse a row of stalls selling reindeer antlers, leather products, fur hats and gloves. A Sami gentleman wearing traditional textiles, a blue *gakti* with embroidered red cloth and a matching cloth hat, stands outside a large tent that houses an indoor market. With striking features, a small nose, red cheeks, narrow eyes and a weathered complexion, he smiles and nods hello. Fascinated by his appearance, Chris asks if we can take his photograph. He kindly agrees and poses proudly for the camera. We greet a woman wearing a dress made from the same traditional embroidered cloth and funky reindeer fur boots. With short mousy brown hair and round spectacles, she sits with a child on her lap, who is clutching a small handmade doll with a reindeer fur hood. The infant turns shyly into his mother. The woman speaks to the gentleman in the Sami language, which has a distinct Nordic rhythm. The guy smiles proudly. We learn he is the woman's father. They ask where we are from and appear pleased to discover we are brothers.

I glance down at the reindeer hides for sale. 'These are yours?'

'Yes, our family. We are herding the reindeer.'

'Do you travel with the animals in the winter, for grazing?'

'These times not so far. The boazovazzi, the reindeer walker, they are using the snowmobiles now.'

Chris turns to the guy. 'What about your father. Did he travel with the reindeer when he was a child?'

'Ja, sure. Today there are many big fences to keep the reindeer inside, but in the old times the people, they had to travel very far away.'

Feeling privileged to meet a traditional Sami family, we invest in a jar of reindeer liver pate and bid these kind gentle people farewell before returning to the road.

Chris looks up from the guidebook. 'Did you know there are eighty-thousand Sami people living in Scandinavia? That's a lot of yoiking.'

'Yoiking?'

'Yep, they can't get enough of it. They yoik in their lavvu tents on cold winter nights, and they even yoik during long sleigh rides across the Arctic tundra. Traditional song is a means of communication and expression. It's one of the oldest continuous musical traditions in Europe. According to oral folklore, the elves of the arctic lands gave yoiks to the Sami people.'

I smile. 'Mythical sprites. I always wondered where they originated from. It's no wonder we imagine Santa Claus to be from around these parts.'

'Absolutely. In fact, it is believed the legend of Santa Claus may have even absorbed elements of Odin.'

'Of course. The Norse mythology god fella with the two ravens on his shoulder.'

'That's the guy,' Chris nods, 'seems very likely when you think about it. Wise old man with a big white beard.'

'What do the Sami people yoik about, anyway?'

'The songs can be deeply personal or spiritual in nature, often dedicated to a human being, an animal or a landscape. Maybe a song about a dog.'

* * *

Producing a deep noise in the throat to show the apparent

emotional content of sorrow or anger, I attempt to sing a yoik song-chant into the wind. Without warning, a white reindeer suddenly hurls itself in front of the car. Si slams on the brakes and our tiny hatchback spins 180 degrees in a half circle. We watch the ghostly albino, with its huge pink antlers, sniff the air. It has the appearance of a mythical creature from a fairytale. Unfazed by its near death experience, the reindeer casually wanders off down the middle of the deserted highway. A toot from the horn sets it running. We follow steadily behind and picking up speed it begins to feel like we are on a sleigh ride. Concerned the animal will panic and bury its head into the window screen, Si gently toots the horn a second time and it leaps majestically into the air and returns to the sanctuary of the forest. We see many more reindeers during our scenic drive. One group congregate in the middle of the road, and look like Dasher, Dancer, Prancer, Vixen, Comet, Cupid, Dunder, Blixem and Rudolph. They all appear to be waiting patiently for Santa to rock up with his sleigh, so they can deliver presents to excited children and have a good time.

We arrive on the island of Kvalsund, and make a pit stop at a viewpoint overlooking the ice-free harbour of Hammerfest.

Si peers over the cliff edge. 'Why Hammerfest? Sounds comedy.'

'The town supposedly has a long history of producing hammers. Every Spring they celebrate the world famous hammer festival.'

'Seriously?'

'Don't be daft.'

'What's the reason, then?'

'Hammer in Old Norse has something to do with large rocks that are good for mooring.'

'You can almost imagine a Viking ship anchored in the bay,' Si smiles. 'Red and white striped sails, bearded horny helmeted warriors unloading barrels of beer onto the shore.'

Winding down the mountain, we drive over a cattle grid that is part of a 20km fence that encircles the town. In the inner parts of Finnmark, herds of up to 3,000 reindeers migrate to the coast from their winter pastures and cause chaos across town. Inside the perimeter fence, I smile at a group of persistent reindeers who have somehow found their way across enemy lines. We park up in the modern red brick centre of a town that has been knocked to the ground multiple times in its recent history. A hurricane flattened Hammerfest in 1856, and then shortly after a fire ripped through the streets. A hundred years was long enough for the town to build itself up again, before the Nazis arrived in their tanks with orders "no building be left standing". We visit the Museum of Reconstruction and feast on information about the history, wildlife and ecology of the area around this arctic community and its uninhabited coast. Si waves me over to a display of black and white photographs depicting the devastation caused here during WWII. We read first-hand accounts from local people who hid in caves in the arctic winter of 1944-45, and thrilling stories stir our imaginations about fishermen battling the ocean waves out at sea. Another great exhibit focuses on the sea life in this region, and we learn about an unusual species of whale that lives off the coast of Svalbard. The Narwhal has a giant three metre long tusk (actually a tooth), which protrudes from the top of its head like an aquatic unicorn. We make a promise to return someday and seek out these fascinating mammals.

Emerging from the museum, we pop into a Joker grocery store and buy a few supplies. At the checkout, Si falls into conversation with a friendly guy with a bulbous nose. He is a little drunk and seems keen to talk to the wind ruffled strangers. Slurring and mumbling, he proceeds to inform us that in addition to Norway, Finland and Sweden, the Sami community also live across the nearby land border with Russia 400km east.

'I was raised in Lovozero close to Murmansk,' he wheezes. 'During Soviet days my great grandfather was forced to move away from the Kola tundra.'

'How many Sami people are there in Russia?' Si asks, paying the cashier.

'Not so many. Less than two-thousand.' He points an accusing finger that is heavily stained by tobacco. 'Not only the Soviet government caused harm to our people, for many years tourists like you travelled to the Kola Peninsula for hunting and fishing. Tourism deprived my people of food and economic livelihood. Large areas of the Ponoi River were stolen from my ancestors.'

'I am sorry to hear that,' Si replies, 'but we're not capable of catching a fish let alone hunting animals like reindeer or moose. So, no trouble here.'

With a bright red face the guy erupts in wheezy laughter. He drunkenly grabs Si in a headlock. 'I make joke, ok? Young travellers like you, we like to see, not the big tourist parties and the hunting tours. We do not want this.'

Wriggling free, Si self-consciously pats his shaggy bouffant and turns to the cashier. She hides her smile and pretends to operate the till. We shake hands with our charismatic new friend, and leave Hammerfest with new appreciation for the hardy people, who inhabit this fascinating region of the extreme Arctic north. On the journey back to the mainland, we debate the impact of mass tourism on the environment, and contemplate the idea of exchanging our petrol engine for pedal power. Si wisely points out that the extreme exertion on our rapidly aging bodies is in itself unsustainable, and would almost certainly lead to cardiac arrest.

* * *

On the banks of Porsangerfjorden, we set up base for the night and build a roaring fire. I am about to crack open a beer when a Volvo estate, with an enormous canoe strapped to the roof, sweeps alongside our hatchback. An athletic woman leaps out of the car.

Her blonde flattop looks golden in the bright sunlight. She marches over to our campfire and fires off a firm salute. Introducing ourselves, we discover Stina is from Gothenburg in the south of Sweden.

Chris offers Stina a beer. 'You have a big canoe!' he smiles.

'Excuse me?'

'The canoe on your car.'

'Oh, yes, sure,' she nods, cracking open the beer.

'I could have sworn there was a big wooden table over there a moment ago.'

Stina laughs in short bursts, revealing powerful arteries in her strong neck. 'So funny! You make joke about the size of my canoe, ja. It must be long, because firstly I am very tall and also the waves they can be very huge in the Arctic sea.'

'You made it yourself?'

'Ja, I am a carpenter. It is for the ocean. Only this morning I was paddling with whales in the Barents Sea. Also, dolphins, seals and many birds taking a ride with me. It was super cool.'

More than happy to meet a new character in the theatre

of our lives, we sit around the campfire in the late evening. We're fascinated to learn that the slight green hue in the sky is in actual fact the northern lights. Stina explains that the aurora can be active anytime of the year, only it is more difficult to see in the summer months, and particularly today as it is the solstice. With a stash of reindeer steaks and a bottle of vodka to share, the evening promises to be memorable. Teaching us how to cook reindeer meat to perfection on the best makeshift campfire grill we have ever seen, we are left feeling completely inspired by the endless skills of wilderness survival that are out there waiting for us to discover.

'I would go camping with my father when I was a child,' Stina smiles, flipping over a steak. 'We also have many beautiful fjords in the south of Sweden. My father taught me how to catch fish and how to make a fire without matches. We even hunted moose together.'

Chris's eyes light up. 'I'd love to see a moose. Everything in the north is so much bigger, the fish, the squid, the eagles and the people.'

'I've been reading a book about Artificial Intelligence,' I smile. 'The author explained that it would be virtually impossible to design a robotic hunter-gatherer. It requires imagination to create stone tools and instinct and ingenuity to track down and catch prey. The skills you need to successfully survive in all climatic conditions are intricate and endless.'

Stina nods vehemently. 'Ja, this is very true. You also need a very powerful sense of taste and smell to avoid eating poisonous mushrooms or plants in the forest. The more time you spend in the wilderness the sharper your instincts become. My niece is studying biology at Uppsala University. She is training to be a doctor.' Stina shows us both a photo of an attractive girl with strawberry blonde hair.

'What's her name?' Chris asks, leaning forward to get a closer look.

'You can't marry her!' Stina laughs. 'Only last week Minna sent me a link to an article about the human nose. I was amazed. There are many hundreds of scent receptors inside. They can detect at least one trillion different smells.'

Chris points at the meat sizzling over the fire. 'There is only one smell in my universe at this moment in time, and it's those juicy reindeer steaks.'

Stina pushes Chris playfully with her powerful arms. 'You British are so funny.'

Raising a toast, the vodka shot burns through my digestive system. 'I guess we are basically animals, like dogs and bears.'

'The fact is, Simon, we have become detached from our natural environment. There is a theory we humans may have lost our sense of smell when we began to walk upright. We lifted our noses away from the earth.' Stina flips the steaks one last time, they sizzle in the heat. 'Please, you can eat.'

Pouncing like an Arctic fox on a plump lemming, Chris presses a steak between two slices of bread and closes his eyes in meat protein ecstasy.

'What interests me the most,' Stina continues, 'is the fact that we humans have a form of echolocation, like bats. You know about this also? When someone who is blind taps a cane on the floor, what they are actually doing is interpreting the sound waves reflected by nearby objects. With training, it is possible to build a mental picture of what is around you. It is very accurate. You can also use clicks or snap the fingers instead. It works the same.'

Chris raises his shot glass. 'Sounds like your superhero

theory, Si.'

'I was thinking the same! Super strength, sight, hearing and smell, we already have these powers, but we rarely get a chance to develop our human potential to its fullest. Our bodies have evolved over millions of years to survive the most extreme environments. Who knows what we are capable of?'

'Ja, this is why I like to kayak the wild oceans. It is the ultimate action movie and more thrilling than the craziest computer game.'

Continuing to debate our realities late into the night, we share stories about our successes and our failings. The chance meeting with Stina has the soothing effect of somehow dismantling any regret we may feel. Stina insists we drink a second, a third and a fourth shot of vodka, until the bottle is empty and all of the reindeer meat has been consumed. Together, the three of us look out across the fjord, red clouds reflected in the mirror surface of the water, three humans whose lives have converged at a single point in time united by a campfire and the pure necessity to rest and eat.

* * *

Menacing storm clouds hover low over the majestic fjord. I see Si sheltering under the golf umbrella in front of a morning fire. I heard Stina strike up her Volvo around six o'clock. Lured by the smell of fresh coffee and fried eggs, I wrestle out of my sleeping bag and collapse out of the car. The words "first light" or "nightfall" have little meaning here in the Arctic north. With all of the time in the world to reach our destination, I use the leftover hot water from breakfast to shave. Si washes in the fjord and slips on a clean shirt. It feels strangely like we are getting ready for a big event, a wedding, a birthday party or a hot date. Throwing the camping equipment into the trunk, we join the E69 on the last road heading north and savour every inch of the highway as we approach the completion of our journey. We hug the coast all the way to the mouth of Porsangerfjorden that opens out into the mighty Barents Sea. On the approach to the North Cape Tunnel, one of the longest subsea road tunnels in Norway, Si toots our comedy horn at a lone hiker with a backpack. Covered in European flags and carrying a banner which reads "Sagres to Nordkapp", we realise the plucky wanderer is approaching the finish line of a five and a half thousand kilometre stroll, from one of the southernmost points of Europe to the most northerly. He doesn't seem in the mood for a chat, so we respect his peace and watch in wonder as he marches towards the conclusion of his great journey. Hurtling below the Magerøysundet strait between the Norwegian mainland and the large island of Magerøya, we wind our way north as the sky blackens. In a torrent of wind and rain, a yellow sign for the Knivskjellodden trail slides into view. We turn sharply down a narrow track and cut the engine.

Si looks out into the mist. 'Hope we don't get attacked by a polar bear or an evil murdering penguin.'

'There aren't any penguins in the Arctic, numbnuts.'

'Since when?'

'Since forever.'

'A penguin and a polar bear have never met?'

My eyes narrow as I suck on a heavily salted chunk of salmiak liquorice, a popular Nordic confectionery. 'Not in the wild. Polar bears live in the northern hemisphere, penguins in the south. They're poles apart.'

3 hours pass...

Shortly after 4pm, the worst of the Arctic storm appears to be over. In normal circumstances it would be insane to consider setting off on a hike this late in the day, but in Northern Norway in the midsummer anytime is trekking time. Si wrestles with his jeans and changes his clothes in the small confines of the hatchback. Inspired by his idea, I too whip a fresh pair of undies out of my rucksack, and perform manoeuvres inside my sleeping bag that would impress even the most talented contortionist. I roll down the window to create more elbow room and inhale an icy breeze.

'Wait a minute!' Si cries, his face frozen with fear. 'These underpants are warm?'

Bursting out of the car, Si's blood-curdling screams echo across the Arctic tundra.

Approaching the start of the trail, I leap up and down on the spot. 'Maybe we should blow some cash, pay the thirty euro entrance fee and enjoy a nice mocaccino in the warm visitors centre.'

'No chance. Time to go that extra mile, buddy,' Si beams, slipping a pair of socks over his hands (he forgot to bring gloves). 'Besides, according to the guidebook, Knivskjellodden will take us further north than the supposed Nordkapp latitude. It will place us at the true extreme northerly point of Europe.'

Using the golf umbrella as a walking stick, we march across the flat, spongy, treeless tundra, with its sharp craggy rocks and boggy puddles. We hit a patch of mist and drift off the trail at various points, but quickly backtrack in a bid to avoid wandering too far in the wrong direction. With only a limited supply of food and water, we are keen not to fall off a cliff and become a minor headline in a local newspaper. We soon begin to descend to the coast and catch a glimpse of the Barents Sea. A large herd of reindeer spill over a nearby ridge and stream down the mountainside. A fearless dotterel sings a warning call from a nearby rock. To our left, a skua swoops low overhead and crashes into a dark blue pond. The Arctic seabird flaps its wings and dips its head under the water before going airborne once more. In the eerie silence it feels like we have been transported back to prehistoric earth. Guided by markers painted on the rocks, we scramble down a steep slope and finally arrive at the open sea. A large white-tailed eagle launches itself off a jagged cliff. Craning our necks we watch as the giant bird of prey glides on the thermals. Navigating deep crevices and stepping cautiously over fragile yellow and pink flowers growing out of cracks in the rocks, we eventually arrive at a pebble beach. A cormorant skims above the ocean and a flock of seagulls cry out a high-pitched Caaa-Caaa. We appear to be completely alone on the trail and the only human beings for miles around. I enjoy the notion that we are possibly the only two people in the whole of mainland Europe at this Arctic latitude at this hour.

'There it is!' Si sings pointing to a pink buoy positioned on top of a concrete plinth.

I look out across the Arctic Ocean as an enormous wave crashes against the rocks. With the North Cape clearly visible to the east, I smile at the thought of our location on the globe. We are now closer in latitude to Greenland and Alaska than the UK. The island of Svalbard is the next big land mass before reaching the North Pole. I imagine the great British explorer Richard Chancellor sailing right past here in 1553 in search of the Northeast Passage. Si dances in celebration around the pink buoy. In an instant it all becomes clear to me. We have completed our quest to drive to the highest point of Europe in our tiny little car. I join my brother in a moment of madness and sing a verse of Sami yoik that drifts across the wild sea.

Road to Damascus in a Ford Escort

On the southern edge of the Jibal al-Alawiyin mountain range, Chris sweeps up to the gates of the 12th century Krak des Chevaliers. Bathed in tangerine light, towers and turrets reach for the sky from the crumbling sandstone block fortress. A flock of sheep crowd around our trusty chariot that has transported us all the way from London to the Middle East. I exchange smiles with a shepherd, who has a black scarf wrapped around his head like a character from an Arabian folktale. With the moon already visible, Chris suggests we spend the night at an inn conveniently located directly beside the castle. From the 650 metre hilltop, we look in awe at Syria below as the adhan (call to prayer) echoes atmospherically across the valley. On the southern flank, directly facing the fort, jagged mountain peaks mark the border with the Lebanon, which as the crow flies is only 10km away from where we are standing.

We are welcomed at the entrance to the inn by a friendly chap with a bushy beard and sparkling eyes black as coal. He is wearing a traditional white cotton throbe that reaches to his ankles. Hassan leads us over to a long table that is occupied by a party of French tourists. Delighted to discover beer is on the menu, Chris quickly orders two bottles of al-Shark, a local brew from Aleppo, along with the restaurant special, lamb kebabs. Waiting for our food to arrive, I fall into conversation with Henri, a serious chap with a ginger goatee and round metal framed glasses. He reveals the group are historians from Strasbourg on a whistle stop tour of Syria and Jordan. The guy sat next to Chris, who we learn is called Eric, speaks only a handful of words in English. He comically uses alcohol as a vehicle for communication.

'Euh, Scotland, whiskey,' he smiles. 'France, wine.'

'England, warm beer,' Chris laughs.

Henri shakes his head. 'Non, non, you have very good beer.'

Eric launches his glass into the air as though it were a medieval goblet or the Cup of Christ. '*À votre santé*!'

We all clink glasses.

'Eric's ancestors, many centuries ago, they travelled here from the Rhine. They were Crusaders and helped to build this castle. Three thousand medieval knights were stationed here. It was one of the Crusader's most important strongholds.'

'Why here?' I ask. 'It seems kind of remote.'

'Whoever controlled this hill dominated the Homs Gap. It is the main passage to Tripoli on the northwest coast of the Lebanon.'

'The Road to Damascus!' Chris sings.

Henri shakes his head. 'Non, non, not exactly. The road to Damascus is the route Saint Paul travelled north from Jerusalem.'

Eric swirls the beer around in his glass to awaken the flavours. He returns Chris's gaze with a display of dancing eyebrows, which has the effect of making us all laugh.

'Who exactly was Saint Paul, an apostle?' I ask.

Henri reaches for a packet of Gauloises. 'Saul of Tarsus was a Jew who converted to Christianity.'

'Isn't Tarsus a city in Turkey?' I ask Henri.

'Yes, it is not so far from here. It was an important Roman city on the Mediterranean coast. He was educated in Jerusalem around the time Jesus was crucified by the Romans.'

'He sounds so grand. Saul of Tarsus. Jesus of Nazareth.'

'Simon of Daventry!' Chris chuckles.

Eric raises a second toast and the table of professors, historians and students respond with a group "*santé*".

The restaurant owner serves tender ground lamb, fresh parsley and a generous helping of hummus.

'*Shukraan*,' Chris beams, practising his Arabic.

Hassan bows before returning to the kitchen.

I turn to Henri. 'So, when Saint Paul converted to Christianity was that a turning point for the Romans?'

Henri waggles a finger. 'Non, non, you must understand, when the Romans first arrived in the Middle East they brought with them their own gods. For many centuries the Romans, the Jews and the powerful ruling families in this region tried to stop the spread of Christianity. It had taken more than three-hundred years before the Romans finally adopted the Christian faith as the official religion of the empire. The prophet Muhammad and the Quran came later in the seventh century.'

Pouring the last valuable drops of the golden beer into our glasses, Eric performs comedy dancing eyebrows for the table one last time before retiring to his room. Chris settles our bill. Appearing regretful that all of the rooms at the inn are occupied, Hassan invites us to sleep on the floor of the restaurant.

'I have two very comfortable mattresses, my friends. You sleep like baby.'

We contemplate the idea of kipping in the car for the night, as we have done many times on our journey across the Balkans and Turkey. Hassan looks concerned. He quietly mentions that only two days ago he heard machine gun fire across the mountains in neighbouring Lebanon.

'Machine gun fire?' I reply. 'Are we safe here?'

'Yes, yes, no problem. Safe.'

Chris rises from the table and speaks in the manner of a Medieval Knight. 'Gentlemen, to bed, for we leave at first light. Tomorrow we ride to Damascus!'

* * *

The clattering of pots and cutlery wakes me with a start. Through bleary eyes, I peer across the restaurant and see our French friends tucking into their breakfast. There is a strong smell of coffee in the air. I cast a wave and the table reply with a hearty "*bonjour*". Si is fast asleep. His blanket has slipped off during the night revealing his pale skin and rather lean physique. Hassan dashes past carrying a tray of freshly cooked eggs. I hurl a rolled up pair of socks at Si's head and he sits up in a daze. His long hair looks wild. To the entertainment of the French diners, we quickly fumble around for our belongings and slip on our t-shirts and jeans.

Feeling a tremendous urge to explore more of this fascinating country, we glide unhindered through the last stretch of the Homs Gap. In the ancient city of Hama, Si locates the perfect picnic spot overlooking the beautiful 300 year old Ottoman Azem Palace, with its iconic wooden

Norias water wheels. Powered by the Orontes River, these elegant wheels were used to irrigate the many acres of orchards and vegetable gardens that once flourished here. Perched on the hood of our electric blue Ford Escort, we feast on chunks of Syrian flatbread stuffed with salty halloumi cheese and plump olives. Palm trees thrive in the lush green gardens on the banks of the river, in a region of the world where settled farming first emerged on the planet. Back on the road, a guy riding a motorcycle speeds past wearing a red and white keffiyeh. These traditional headdresses are commonly worn in this region of the Middle East to protect the face from dust, sand and sunburn.

'Lawrence of Arabia!' Si howls, his eyes widening as he swerves to avoid a ten-ton truck travelling the wrong way up the highway.

Approaching the city of Homs, a road sign whips overhead in both English and Arabic directing traffic to Beirut 181km southwest and Baghdad 844km east. The landscape is dry and barren. Over 3,000 years ago, a great battle was fought here between the Egyptians and the Hittites. An astonishing 6,000 chariots were believed to have been involved. That's a lot of hoof and mane. Without warning the front right tyre suddenly blows. Si wrestles with the steering wheel and sharply exits the highway onto a gravel track. We skid up alongside a whitewashed stone building covered in Arabic writing. It is our second puncture in less than a week. Jacking up the car we battle in the heat to fit the spare wheel in place. Thankfully the axle bolt is still tight, after a mechanical issue in Turkey led to us spending the night in a hotel reminiscent of the psychological horror *The Shining*. I decide to capture our road trip breakdown moment on camera, set the timer and leap into view. As we squint in the bright sunlight, a black Nissan exits the highway and glides slowly past. A group of guys eyeball us with suspicion. A wave of paranoia washes over me. War has been raging in nearby Iraq for four years now. With Baghdad located only 750km away from our chosen destination of Damascus, it all feels uncomfortably close.

Back on the road, we look out across the Syrian Desert that occupies an incredible fifty-five percent of the country. Hike east from here and it is drier than a lizard's whistle for over three hundred kilometres, all the way to the Euphrates River in Iraq. To the west of the road the Anti-Lebanon Mountains rise steeply above us. Si swerves sharply around a cement mixer that has buried itself into a bridge. We ease up on the gas and cruise towards the city of Damascus beneath a glorious blue sky. The popular hit "Toos Rap" by Iranian rapper Yas blasts from the car stereo. We begin to see enormous billboards of the president Bashar al-Assad. Since arriving in Syria, virtually every vehicle and shop window across the country appears to display a sticker or poster of the president. Politics in this region it seems has grown more authoritarian in recent years, with the People's Council of Syria only last week voting in Assad for a second term.

Rolling through the suburbs of the oldest continuously inhabited city in the world, a road sign appears for the "oPt" (a term used by the UN to describe Palestinian territory occupied by Israel). Si's driving skills are tested to their limits as he battles with our fellow road users. I exchange curious glances with the driver of a red Suzuki hatchback, who is wearing a white kufi prayer cap and has a well kempt silky grey beard. Without a hotel booked, we agree to simply follow signs to Damascus Old Town and hunt around for somewhere to ditch the car. Entering the historic quarter, I clench my butt cheeks as the road narrows way beyond our comfort levels. Nudging through a stretch of the ancient covered souq, exotic spices, incense and fine cotton textiles are within easy reach. Folding in the wing mirrors, Si turns fearlessly into a crowded side street. His brave manoeuvre pays off and we are shot like a cannon ball out of the old city walls and into the fast flow of the traffic.

'Parking space!' I yell.

Slamming on the brakes, an angry taxi driver shakes his fist in the air. Si lowers his gaze until the volume of car horns subsides. Sweat streams down his face as he reverses into the tiny gap between two cars. A guy wearing baggy suit trousers slides up besides us. Happy to recruit this friendly fella to keep an eye on the Escort during our time in Damascus, Si dives into his wallet and spins him a couple of dollars. We march across a footbridge to the commercial centre. In contrast to the traditional kaftans, burkas, hijabs and keffiyehs worn by local folk in the souq, in this part of town smartly dressed office workers roam the streets. A woman exits a bank with a clipboard in her hand, her thick curly hair is uncovered and bleached blonde. Si nudges my arm and points out a guy with a handgun tucked into the back of his jeans. His serious demeanour suggests he could be a plain clothed police officer, or work in government security. On the fringes of the Old City we duck inside a three star hotel, but rather abruptly get turned away. We try three more similar budget options on the same street with no success. We begin to suspect the hoteliers are not allowed to legally accommodate foreigners. I catch a glimpse of my reflection, five days beard growth sprouts from my face. Si's mane of hair is seriously out of control. With sunburnt cheeks, scruffy t-shirts and dusty backpacks slung over our shoulders, at first glance you would be forgiven for thinking we had just hiked across the desert from Baghdad. Fishing out our smartest clothes we freshen up in the toilets of a café. Buzzing from strong Arabic coffee, Si lashes his hair back in a ponytail and suggests we try one of the more expensive hotels. After all, we have saved cash on fuel with a litre of gasoline in Syria cheaper than a can of Coca Cola.

* * *

From the marble and chrome lounge of our sky rise hotel, an Arabian sheikh watches our clumsy attempt at hailing a cab. Growing impatient, Chris leaps into the middle of the road and waves his arms in the air. A classic Mercedes taxi screeches to a halt and we bundle inside. Asking the friendly driver to take us to Jabri House, he expertly negotiates a maze of narrow backstreets. Sweeping through an alleyway that is barely the width of the car we applaud Farid, who seems relieved not to have become wedged between two ancient stone walls. We draw up outside a traditional Ottoman house built in 1737. A young waiter wearing a waistcoat leads us to a table on a balcony that overlooks the beautiful covered courtyard. He immediately serves mint tea and a mixed platter of walnuts, almonds and pistachio nuts. Above the small stage an enormous black and white arch frames an ornate lantern. Pillars and even the walls are similarly constructed from alternating courses of white limestone and black basalt in typical Damascene architectural style. Chris orders a giant double nargilah pipe. The waiter uses metal tongs to balance a couple of cubes of hot charcoal on top of the foil-covered ceramic neck of the pipe. Drawing hard on one of the hoses that protrude from the hookah, we hear the satisfying sound of air bubbling inside the bulbous glass base and the sizzle of moist tobacco as the coals glow red. We disappear in a veil of smoke. Mesmerized by music performed on an oud, the talented musician shifts up a gear and begins to strum a lively traditional song. A guy wearing a fitted purple shirt springs to his feet and begins to stamp his shiny shoes in time with the beat. Reminiscent of a male flamenco dancer or a matador at a bullfight, with outstretched arms he oozes confidence as he rotates slowly in a circle. Our food arrives, and we devour the grilled skewers of chicken and lamb with peppers. Pita bread dipped in creamy hummus dissolves in our mouths. The freshness of raw cucumber, red onion, carrot and radish, garnished with lemon, garlic, olive oil and mint leaves works its magic to deliver us to culinary heaven.

Wandering through the atmospheric cobbled streets to the Christian Quarter around Bab Tuma, we make a beeline for a watering hole on the corner of Mar Mar. Chris orders Johnnie Black on the rocks to celebrate our arrival in Damascus. We fall into conversation with a guy from the Netherlands and his girlfriend, and discover this plucky couple have travelled overland by public transport from Egypt. Fabian has been studying International Politics in Cairo and Hannah recently completed a PhD in Agricultural Science in Utrecht. A larger than life guy smoking a big cigar leans into our conversation. We discover he is a fashion designer from Dubai. He asks what we think of Damascus and is pleased by our stories of the exceptional Middle Eastern hospitality. Insisting we join him for a drink, he orders a round of cocktails and proceeds to entertain Chris and Fabian with videos on his iphone of Arabian fashion models. Hannah proceeds to blow my mind with scientific theories about what may have caused humans to first start farming in the Fertile

Crescent.

'I wrote my thesis around the subject of the Sahara pump theory,' Hannah smiles. 'It's not sexual in any way.'

'What's it about?' I smile.

'It's totally boring.'

'I love this stuff. Indulge me.'

'Ok. Well, you have to think of the Middle East as a land bridge between Africa and Eurasia. Over thousands of years this region of the world experienced countless climatic changes. The Sahara was wet and covered in giant lakes and rivers numerous times in the ancient past.'

'Lakes?'

'Yep, picture mangrove forest, marshes and grassland. According to the theory, instead of wooded growth these major climatic changes from wet Sahara to dry Sahara may have favoured the evolution of plants that die off annually and produce edible seeds.'

'So, what you're basically saying is that humanity, modern culture, written language, civilization as we know it, may have only become possible with the arrival of seed based crops?'

'It's a little more complicated than that, Simon, but, yes. There is evidence humans have been collecting and snacking on wild grain for at least one hundred thousand years. Cultivation came later, with the first crops being farmed in the Levant and rice in China around twelve thousand years ago.'

'I guess it's no coincidence that soon after we began to see the emergence of modern religions.'

'Exactly! Farming enabled humans to live in much larger groups. We formed the first towns and cities and developed sophisticated belief systems.'

Our conversation is suddenly interrupted by a confident young guy wearing bright red trousers. He grabs Hannah by the hand and spins her onto the dance floor. With the Arabic dance music at full volume, I find myself unable to resist a little light footwork. Impressed by the energy of a liberal crowd of Middle Eastern revellers, I cut a rug with a beautiful Jordanian woman, who I discover is celebrating her Hen weekend. Fixing me with feline eyes we dance without touching, her arms snaking above her head in the manner of an Egyptian belly dancer.

* * *

Weaving through the Al-Hamidiyah souq, Si waves me over to a tamr hendi vendor. Wearing a crimson fez hat, the guy acrobatically fills two small glasses with juice from a tall silver vase-shaped vessel. The tart tasting tamarind helps soothe an aggressive hangover. We mooch around the shops and stalls and stock up on spices, tea and incense. Powered by sticky Arab sweets and pastries, we admire finely woven carpets and sparkling gold jewellery. Emerging from the souq, we blink in the bright sunlight as we approach the beautiful Umayyad Mosque. Completed in 715, Si reveals the Great Mosque was the first building of significant size and importance in Islamic history and was built on the ruins of a church soon after the Muslim conquest of Damascus. It is fascinating to discover that layers of religious belief have existed on this very spot for an incredibly long period of time. In recorded history, a temple once stood here 3,000 years ago, belonging to an ancient tribal confederation known as the Arameans. Later, during Roman rule a temple for the worship of Jupiter enjoyed its heyday. Next the arrival of Christianity saw it rebuilt for at least the third time as a church dedicated to John the Baptist. With a notepad and pen in his hand, Si gazes in awe at the Dome of the Eagle, located atop the centre of the main prayer hall. We wander in silence over to an opulent shrine that is alleged to contain the head of John the Baptist. A few years ago, Pope John Paul II visited the shrine and became the first ever supreme pontiff of the Roman Catholic Church to set foot inside a mosque. Si reveals the execution of John the Baptist was ordered by King Herod, the Roman client king, during the same period Jesus was crucified. John was recognised by all those faithful to him as a prophet and is considered by some religious groups to be the forerunner for Jesus, as he anticipated the coming of a messianic figure greater than himself. Outside the prayer hall, Si enthusiastically identifies one of three minarets where Muslims believe Jesus will return to Earth at the End of Days. Dazzled by great legends, we visit the spectacular As'ad Pasha Caravanserai. Hidden deep within the Al-Buzuriyyah souq, we are blown away by the black and white ablaq Damascene palace that once hosted camel caravans travelling from across the Middle East. We relax in the shade and people watch. Children dance in a water fountain, shoppers haggle and day trippers take selfies with UN soldiers. I snap a photo of Si standing in front of a statue of the mighty Saladin on horseback. Described during his reign as the de facto Caliph ruler of Islam, Saladin led the Muslim military campaign in the 12th century against the Crusader states and was the first Sultan of Egypt and Syria. A guy in his twenties standing on scaffolding whistles down and asks to have his photograph taken. Covered in dust and wearing a keffiyeh, he poses with a cigarette hanging from his bottom lip like a 1950s movie star.

On our way back to the hotel we bump into Fabian. He looks incredibly hungover.

'Hannah is in bed,' he croaks, rubbing his tired eyes.

'We had a big fight last night. She wanted to leave the bar before it closed. How was I supposed to know? I'm not a mind reader. Anyway, I was drunk. Come on, join me for coffee. I need coffee.'

Entering a nearby cafe, we are surprised to be welcomed inside by the young guy Amir from the Lebanon, who danced with Hannah in the bar last night.

'Simon! I thought you leave today?'

'No, we changed our minds in the end. There's too much to see here.'

I shake Amir by the hand. 'Hey, you're the character from a storybook.'

Amir laughs, tiny tremors causing his fashionable black framed spectacles to leap about his face. 'I often say this when I am drinking beer.'

'Well, I guess you are wearing red trousers. Surely only a character from the pages of a mythical fantasy wears red trousers.'

'I'm Hannah's boyfriend,' Fabian smiles.

Amir appears embarrassed. 'I hope I did not offend you.'

'No problem. In the Netherlands it is the woman who chooses to marry not the man.'

Everyone laughs with the exception of a thickset guy wearing a suit jacket, who rises from a table in the corner of the café. He eyeballs me with suspicion.

'You are from Britain?'

'Yes,' I smile. The guy declines my offer of a handshake and instead flattens his moustache with his thumb and index finger.

'What is it with this Tony Blair? More than a million Iraqi refugees in Syria now. Baghdad is destroyed.'

Si steps forward. 'We have good friends in the UK, refugees from Mosul in the north of Iraq.'

'Kurdish?' The guy glares.

Si nods mutely.

The guy looks fit to explode, a smart proud man it seems clear he has a deep need to vent his anger.

'Bush and Blair are your leaders. They should be thrown in the jail.'

Slapping a few coins on the table he leaves with a grunt.

Amir breaks the silence. 'Pizza? The homemade pizza here is very good. You want to try? Please, I insist you try.'

'Do you own this place, Amir?' I ask, slightly shaken by the rather volatile encounter with an unhappy local.

'No, no, the owner asked me to look for him. He needed to go to the market. He returns soon. I am a tourist like you. We are all brothers here in the Middle East.'

'Are you Sunni Muslim?'

'No, I am a Christian. You bought me a beer!'

'I did wonder about that,' Si smiles. 'Are there many Christians in the Lebanon?'

'Around forty percent. We are the most religiously diverse country in the Middle East.'

'Life would be so much easier if everyone abandoned religion,' Fabian sighs.

Amir looks serious for a moment. 'That is what the Soviets thought, but you cannot force people to abandon their beliefs.'

'True, but it is frustrating all the same. Religion breeds such willing soldiers.'

'You don't need religion for that. I remember kids at school locking arms and marching around the playground. They would all chant together, "who wants to play army". Other boys would join and the gang would grow until the bell rang. Tribalism is buried deep within our DNA.'

Fabian's face lights up. 'Hannah has been teaching me about cognition. It's now understood that it was only when humans evolved the ability to imagine, that it was possible for large groups to unite around belief in a god or a nation under one flag. If only humanity could agree to unite under one single ideology. We should invent one.'

Si shakes his head vehemently. 'I think humans will always end up fighting over who gets to rule the world.'

Hannah appears in the doorway to the café. 'Man party?' She asks. 'Are women allowed in here?'

'Only to eat pizza,' Fabian beams, offering her a rectangular slice as though it were Cinderella's slipper.

She accepts the gift and cosies up beside him. It seems clear all has been forgiven.

Amir looks sheepishly down at his shoes.

'So, what have you been talking about?'

Fabian casts her a sideways glance. 'We're attempting to solve humanities problem of this never-ending cycle of war and violence. Any idea what we should do?'

Hannah hesitates before answering. 'Yes,' she nods. 'In fact, I know exactly the solution.'

'What is it?' we all sing in unison.

With lightning reactions, she snatches a knife from the pizza tray and trusts it into the air. 'Cut off the balls of every man.'

Africa in Gujarat

Thundering through the dead of night beneath an ocean of stars, I begin to contemplate the insanity of our mission.

'Ready to meet lion?' our guide Raju yells over the noise of the jeep.

'Eaten by lion?' Si cries, his scruffy hair whipping above his head. 'I sincerely hope not Raju!'

Rescued from the brink of extinction, the Gir National Park is the last remaining territory of the rare Asiatic lion. Fearing our guide Raju may be sharing information crucial to our survival, I strain to hear as he continues to talk animatedly over his shoulder with the appearance of a character in a silent movie. I flash a smile at Si and our good friend Darell. We all raise our thumbs with excitement. The jeep slows to a crawl and Raju flicks on a powerful spotlight. Acrobatic bats dart overhead. He angles the beam to reveal two jackals with dusty grey coats standing proudly over a spotted deer. Not wishing to disturb the wildlife for long, we continue a short distance before swerving sharply onto an unpaved track. We skid to a halt outside a single storey farmhouse. Greeted by a woman wearing a pink sari, we are ushered into a walled backyard and offered tea. We look in surprise when our host wanders over to a large water buffalo munching on hay, and begins milking the animal directly into a saucepan.

'Now that's what you call fresh,' Si laughs.

She adds tea and sugar and boils the brew over a hot stove. Raju demonstrates how to drink the lively chai Gujarati style. He pours the sweet tea into a saucer, and cools the liquid by swirling it around. We are introduced to a local guy called Munjal and his children, who dance excitedly around the buffalo.

'Munjal will be joining us tonight,' Raju informs us. 'A lion killed a cow not far from here. We are waiting for its exact location.'

Si leans forward. 'Are we in any danger?'

'The outcome, sir, depends on numerous factors.' Raju pauses to light a beedi, a small Indian cigarette hand rolled from a tobacco leaf. We are left on tenterhooks. Raju exhales the tobacco smoke and it spirals into the humid air. 'Firstly, you must understand,' he continues, 'I can almost one hundred percent guarantee that you will not be eaten by a lion.'

'Almost?'

'We need a Rhodesian Ridgeback,' I suggest to the group. 'They were bred in Africa to keep lions at bay.'

'Hate to break this to you, Chris, but we're not in Africa.'

'The Ridgeback is very strong,' Raju nods, 'but here in Sasan we are not scared of the lions. You show you are scared, maybe you have trouble. The leopard is different. We're scared of the leopard.' Raju sinks his long nails into Si's shoulder causing him to dribble tea down his chin. 'The leopard attacks from the trees. They can sometimes be seen around the farm.' He points an accusing finger at me. 'You snore loudly in the night time?'

'Yes, yes, he does,' Si nods vehemently. 'Like a warthog!'

Our friend Darell bursts out laughing.

'If you snore like a pig it attracts the leopards.'

'I only snore when I've been drinking. It's my adenoids.'

Si rolls his eyes. 'More like your fat neck-anoids.'

'What are leopards and lions doing around here, anyway?' I ask. 'I thought we were on the perimeter of the national park?'

'Sasan Gir is not a zoo, sir. The home of the animals is also outside the core protected area. There are over eighty villages in this region in total. The animals live very close to farms and the people.'

'Similar to the jackals we saw earlier,' Si adds.

'Yes, sir, we have many cobras, also pythons. They hide in the long grass. Only a few years ago, a man was swallowed by a very big python not far from here. He was sleeping outside. The snake took him, but he was still holding onto his camel. The camel ran away and dragged him into the village.'

'Still inside the snake?'

'Yes, he was inside. The local people they killed the snake. Unfortunately, it was not possible to save him.'

Munjal appears in the doorway, and nods. Raju claps his hands together. 'Ok, now you ready to see lion?' he grins.

Squeezing aboard the jeep, we travel to the north side of the national park and pull over next to a ploughed field.

Raju speaks in a hushed voice. 'You have been very lucky. The lions killed the farmer's cow only an hour ago. For sure we see lion tonight. The farmer moved the cow away from his house with a tractor. The lions will be looking for their kill, so we have to be quick. It is a short walk across this field.'

Si frowns. 'Hang on, did you say, "walk"?'

'Yes, we walk to the kill. Please, the lions will be here soon. We must go now!'

I jump out of the jeep and turn to Raju. 'If you don't mind me asking, where is your gun?'

'We do not have permission for firearms. I have my stick.'

'A stick?'

'Please, we go!'

In the light of a crescent moon we stumble across a ploughed field, the reality of what we are doing is difficult to fathom. I calm myself with the thought that although Raju is not exactly an official guide, he grew up in Sasan and has spent his life living alongside the wildlife. He also appears intelligent, sound of mind and not suicidal in the slightest, which is excellent news. We approach the carcass of a large muscular cow lying in a heap on its side. I admire the animal's impressive curved horns. The flesh around its throat has been completely torn open, and the tough skin on its hide is shredded and clawed away exposing the fresh red meat below. Raju takes a quick turn around the animal and scans the ground for pugmarks.

'The lion, she attacked from behind and then grabbed the throat.'

'Was it more than one lion?' Si asks.

'No, it looks like only one made the kill.'

I feel incredibly vulnerable in the wide open space. There is literally nowhere to run and hide. Raju also looks nervous. He taps Munjal on the shoulder and the men whisper in Gujarati.

He turns to us with haunting eyes. 'Yes, we go now,' he whispers. 'The lions will not want to share their food with the jackals and hyenas.'

* * *

A loud snort frightens me awake. Squeezed into the rear of the Gypsy jeep I lean away from Chris, only to recoil at the sight of Darell to my right. Wrestling free, I hurl myself out of the open top 4x4. The two weary travellers collapse into each other.

Raju skips over. 'You have cigarette for the park guard?'

I whip a couple of Gold Flakes out of Darell's jacket pocket.

Raju returns moments later. 'The park gates are closed during the night, so we will be the first vehicle on the trail.'

The roar of the engine shakes Chris and Darell into action. I nod good morning to the smart park official, who has a rifle slung over his shoulder and a bristly moustache. With the sun flickering behind the trees, the world of Sasan Gir explodes into life. The echoing cry of a peacock deep within the forest is accompanied by flashes of blue from the bright wings of a kingfisher. Raju skilfully points out graceful chinkara gazelles camouflaged in the forest, as a family of mongoose scurry through the long grass beside a sambar deer. Since 1965, Gir National Park has been a sanctuary for the last remaining Asiatic lions that call these dry, deciduous forests home. In 1913, there were only 55 of these big cats remaining, but today thanks to a successful breeding program there are now over 500. Up until the 19th century, the territory of the Asiatic lion stretched as far east as Bihar with the last sightings recorded near Delhi in 1834 and in Rajasthan in 1870.

We pass a small group of wooden houses nestled in the forest. 'This is one of the villages inside the park,' Raju smiles beneath his mirrored sunglasses. 'Maaldharis live here. They are cattle herders.'

Raju waves to a local nomad driving a herd of water buffalo. The elderly gentleman is wearing traditional white woven cotton, of the kind worn by Mahatma Gandhi, and he has a face baked by the sun. The nomad points towards railway tracks running through the trees that carry trains across the national park to the southern coast of Gujarat three hours away.

'He saw a lion half an hour ago,' Raju translates.

'Isn't he afraid?' Chris asks.

'No, this is normal for him. He lives with the lions. They do not want to eat people they are only interested in the cattle.'

It seems insane that this nomad would herd his cattle through lion territory, but the villagers have little choice. For centuries their livelihoods have depended on foraging for fuel. With rapidly declining areas of forest outside the parks boundaries, they must share what remains with these endangered big cats.

'If a cow is taken the cattle herder is given money by the government,' explains Raju. 'They do this so the local people do not harm any lions.'

Wrestling the frustration of having yet to encounter the elusive Gir lion, we return to the guesthouse for lunch. We sit in the shade of the porch and tuck into a delicious feast of rice, dhal, vegetables, chapati, papadum and curd. Chatting to the young owner Nitin, we discover he has been offering accommodation in his family's home and jeep tours of Sasan Gir for a number of years now. Nitin started out in his career selling peanuts and snacks to the passing traffic. One afternoon a tourist from Europe arrived by bus and asked if there was a guest house nearby. Nitin invited the young backpacker to stay at his home. More foreigners began to arrive, and very quickly he found he had a new business. With his own motorbike and a team of guides at his disposal, Nitin today is clearly a successful entrepreneur. Last year, he built three new rooms to rent to tourists at the foot of his garden, complete with en-suite bathroom. Appearing keen for us to have the best experience possible, Nitin calls a few friends and organises a hike. He promises we will not leave Sasan without seeing a lion. With time to kill, Chris suggests we visit an African community that live a twenty minute ride away. Our auto-rickshaw, powered by a 500cc Royal Enfield motorcycle, skids into the village of Jambut. We learn the Siddi are an ethnic Swahili group, who are descendants of the Bantu peoples of East Africa. Arriving at a local home, we are invited to watch a man and his son dance the Dhamal, which is traditionally performed in Africa after a successful hunting expedition. Wearing tribal jewellery and headdresses, they dance to pounding drums and the beat of the dhol, also known as the mushaira. For over 300-years the Siddi have lived peacefully in this remote corner of India. They adopted the Muslim religion, but still hold on to their language and cultural identity. Our guide explains that the people here believe they originate from Uganda, and for centuries they have made a living working the fields. We wander around the main square where a group of Siddi women wearing colourful saris and headscarves are playing cards, and we peer through the gates of a beautiful mosque covered in turquoise mosaic tiles. Chris and Darell spice up our lives with deep fat fried chilli peppers at a street stall. A local guy rocks up with a one-day-old parrot chick nestled in the palm of his hand. A group of kids gather around, but they seem more interested in the foreigners than the blind, featherless bird. We join them in a round of selfies.

Bidding the village farewell, we continue with our mission to encounter an Asiatic lion. As the afternoon heat intensifies, we hike to the perimeter of the national park and wade across a river to the forest where brittle twigs snap underfoot. A colony of gray langur monkeys watch curiously from the trees. To the untrained eye our surroundings look virtually the same in every direction. I feel thankful to be led by Raju and a second local guide, who appears to know exactly where he is going. We fight through thick foliage close to a swamp that is allegedly home to a mugger crocodile.

'Think we'll see anything?' Chris smiles, using his t-shirt to wipe sweat from his face.

'Surely this has got to be a wild-goose chase,' I reply, fishing a bottle of water out of my bag. 'I like Raju and Nitin, but I'm beginning to suspect they simply haven't got permits to guide us properly around the core of the national park.'

On the far side of the swamp our guide stops sharply in his tracks and blocks the way ahead with outstretched arms. Raju points to a tree less than twenty metres away. I am expecting to see a sambar deer or maybe another monkey. My jaw hits the ground when my blurred vision focuses on two male lions. They fix us with a hard stare. I can hardly believe my eyes. My brain screams at me, "run for your life, you idiot!", but I find my legs remain completely frozen to the spot.

Raju stands casually with his hands on his hips like he has just pointed out a squirrel. 'Lion,' he beams. 'You see, I told you we would see lion.'

The ranger turns to us and puts a finger to his lips.

Raju lowers his voice to a whisper. 'We must stay quiet and still. The lions, they are sleepy in the heat and have just eaten a buffalo. We don't want to disturb them.'

Silence screams out among us when one of the lions slowly rises to its feet, revealing its sheer size. It has a short mane, sparse and darker compared to the African lion. Folds of skin run the length of its belly. The beast yawns displaying a mean pair of incisors. Images flash through my mind of being torn limb from limb, our intestines flung about all over the jungle. I picture a no-frills tombstone, the inscription reads, "Here lie the savaged remains of the Raven Brothers and their best mate. They got eaten by a lion." Raju stands with his back to the animals and poses with Chris and Darell for a series of photographs for his social media profile. I find I am unable to relax. With similar moves to a domestic kitty, the lethargic lion walks around in a tight circle before slumping back down onto the forest floor. With the photo session over, we return through the Gir forest and leave these wild animals to enjoy their afternoon siesta. The experience of gazing into the eyes of a wild Asiatic lion is engraved permanently in our memories. Here in Gujarat is a slice of Africa, complete with lions, leopards, crocodiles, jackals, hyenas and a thriving African community. Sasan is a natural paradise brimming with personality, where good people live side by side with nature, and where the creation of a wildlife sanctuary continues to stand strong against the pressure of humans' thirst for land.

Into Spain's Wild West

Trapped between sliding doors at the entrance to a Spa supermarket, Si struggles free. He eyeballs me over rock star shades. 'Do we seriously need all of this stuff? The shopping bags are already cutting into my fingers.'

'I hope you're not going to moan the entire seventy-five kilometres to Mérida. This isn't the Camino de Santiago with burger joints on route. This is the real deal. Proper adventure. We could die out there.'

'Four litres of boxed wine?'

I crack a smile. 'It's juice. We need to keep our sugar levels up. Besides, I'm on holiday.'

A wooden gatepost on the fringes of Cáceres marks kilometre one of our challenging quest. Facing the arrow-straight trail that cuts across a field of golden wheat, I take the opportunity to limber up and perform a series of star jumps. With the growing popularity of the Camino de Santiago in recent years, it hadn't taken Si much persuasion to join me on a two-day hike of this less visited region of the Spanish interior. We are out of shape and unprepared. This is going to be an adventure. Launching ourselves onto the Via de la Plata (Silver Way), we quickly lose ourselves in the idyllic rural setting of the

Extremadura. Escaping hectic city life for a few days, we are immediately zapped into a world of gigantic skies where black kites, swifts and swallows and colourful butterflies welcome us along the trail. Approaching a small farmhouse, we greet a stocky dog chained to a fence made of rusty bedsprings. Four magnificent Andalusian horses graze in a nearby field. Si feeds the pregnant mare an apple. In the shade of a tree, the three younger horses are standing head to rear and appear to work as a team to waft away the flies from their eyes and nostrils. I wrestle the sudden urge to leap onto the back of the brown colt in the middle and gallop to Mérida like a fearless cowboy. Two of the most famous conquistadors from Spain were born in this region of the Extremadura; Francisco Pizarro, who conquered the Inca Empire in Peru, and Hernán Cortés whose expedition led to the collapse of the Aztec Empire. The horses they used during their perilous journeys were of course Andalusian, a breed known for their stamina and unnerving intelligence. It had been the arrival of the Moorish cavalry a thousand years ago, that led to the creation of this new super breed. In addition to importing radical new riding and battle techniques, the North African's bred their Barb horses with the native Iberian creating a new war horse that was to impact the world for centuries to come. With more chance of destroying the soles of our feet rather than innocent civilizations, we continue on our mission to Mérida.

Ten kilometres south of Cáceres we reach a sign warning of a military zone. Free of tanks and heavy artillery, the deserted trail continues to wind across virgin countryside. Si points out flashes of colour as bee-eaters, hoopoes and European rollers dart between the olive trees. Weaving around red-striped oil beetles that dot the trail, we push past the quiet village of Valdesalor and march across rolling hills that stretch to the horizon. In the middle of nowhere, we cross an impressive 2,000 year-old Roman segmental arch bridge. I try to imagine soldiers, traders and pilgrims, who would have travelled this ancient route many centuries ago. On the far side of an abandoned aerodrome, we observe a field of black Iberian pigs feasting in an orchard of acorns, a technique used in the production of Spain's highly prized jamón ibérico de bellota.

Si shoots a sideways grin. 'Guess how much the most expensive leg of ham in the world costs?'

'Left or right? Front or rear?'

'No idea,' Si laughs.

'Three-hundred quid?'

'And the rest.'

'Five-hundred quid?'

'Try four-thousand euros.'

'Seriously?'

'The Manchado de Jabugo is a rare breed. Apparently, they're encouraged to forage for acorns and almonds and root around in the woodlands washed by Atlantic rains.'

Beyond the orchard of pigs we stumble across a herd of sandstone horned milkers. They eyeball us over an electrified fence. From out of nowhere a huge bull appears. It snorts and drags its foot through the dust.

'Avoid eye contact!' I yell, marching quickly past with the shopping bags swinging vigorously either side of my big banana feet.

The muscular bull releases a rather alarming elongated bellow, before charging furiously alongside the flimsy fence.

'Holy fuck, I'm wearing red checks!' Si hollers.

We hide a safe distance from the half ton beast in a cluster of oak trees.

* * *

A sheep traffic jam stops us in our tracks. More than fifty of the beige woolly animals fill the path forcing us to fight our way through. A shepherd stands nearby and watches his flock. He acknowledges Chris's cheerful *"buenos tardes!"* with a friendly nod. Purple thistles and a stone bridge welcome us on the approach to the small rural community of Aldeo del Cano. On the fringes of town we pass a boarded up nightclub called Pecado, which rather curiously is the Spanish word for sin. A faded neon sign, with the silhouette of two dancing girls, suggests this creepy looking establishment may have at one time accommodated ladies of the night. Wandering along the main street there isn't anyone around. In fact, apart from the shepherd, we haven't seen a single soul the entire day. I begin to wonder if this is how it might feel to live in a post-apocalyptic world. A stork nesting high on the top of a church tower peers down at us. I catch myself nodding hello. Making a loop around the village, Chris pauses in front of a faded poster advertising a bullfight in the nearby village of Montanchez.

'My dogs are barking,' he sighs, whipping off a running shoe and massaging his swollen foot. 'We could seriously use Uber Camino right now. Hey, look, a café!'

With aching limbs we zombie over to a scruffy snack bar. Chris throws his shopping bags to the ground and orders two large beers. A local woman with a pierced eyebrow serves olives, oily diced chorizo sausage and a fat slice of homemade Spanish tortilla. The ice cold Cerex beer disappears down our throats at rapid speed. We quickly order two more. We fall into conversation with a deeply tanned gentleman who sports magnificent sideburns.

77

Javier is a friendly chap and, using our basic Spanish, we discover that he used to deliver fruit and vegetables to towns along this once major road in Western Spain. The construction of the new superfast Autovía-66, linking Salamanca in the north of Spain with Seville in the south, had diverted away much of the through traffic. Javier appears nostalgic for the old times when the small rural communities in this region were full of life. An overweight guy wearing a neck brace joins Javier at the table. He exhales black cigarillo smoke in between sips of brandy, and eyeballs us with suspicion. Fed and watered, we wish Javier good luck and continue our hike in the cool evening air. Chris locates a lake not too far away where we can set up camp for the night. Skimming alongside a dry stone wall, we cross a field under the watchful eye of a golden eagle. It soars above us, all the way to the lake's welcoming shores. Before we have even had a chance to sit down, Chris has the wine open. Snacking on a jar of stuffed olives we witness Earth's spectacle, as the peach sky dissolves into night.

'We made it off-grid, hippie boy.' Chris raises his paper cup in a toast and knocks back the sharp tasting wine.

'It feels kind of strange to be sitting here without a tent. Shelter is top priority in most survival emergencies.'

'This isn't an emergency,' Chris laughs. 'It's the beginning of summer. No rain tonight.'

'What if a sheep chews off my face while I'm sleeping?'

'Absolutely no problem at all, with modern technology these days you can easily get a new one.'

'I don't want a new one. I like the face I have.'

'But you look like a poorly paid Mick Jagger impersonator.' Chris darts a paranoid glance over his shoulder.

'What is it?'

'I thought I heard a scream.'

'That doesn't sound good.'

'It came from the field behind. Maybe that freaky guy from the café followed us here.'

'The dude with the neck brace?'

'No, he was wearing an army jacket. Stick thin, greasy long hair.' Chris refills the cups and looks up at the sky. 'It's almost full moon.'

'Oh great, that night of the month when all manner of devils come out to play.'

'Maybe we should build a fire.'

'Won't that draw the attention of the village people?'

Chris busts open a sack of tortilla chips. 'I seriously doubt a troupe of aging American disco stars would be travelling all the way out here in the Extremadura.'

'Not those village people.' I take a moment to flick through the small notebook that I carry around in my back pocket.

'Write any good lines recently?'

'One movie idea we could work on.'

'Don't tell me, is it a dark psychological horror?'

'Nope, comedy drama.'

'Comedy? Are you sure?' he smirks. 'What's it about?'

'A forklift truck competition.'

'Brilliant. That's actually kind of unique. What else have you got in that little black book of thoughts?'

'It's a mixed bag. How about a movie line for a Western? Think Clint Eastwood.' I narrow my eyes like a cowboy. '"The only reason I wash my jeans is to keep the pockets tight." I also wrote a poem.'

'When?'

'On the train to Cáceres. It poured out of me in a stream of consciousness. It's a rough draft.' I straighten my posture and clear my throat. I begin to read. 'We all have to come to terms with the fact we are alone and the audience exists only in our imagination. The Earth moves solidified beneath our feet and we feel nauseous with the motion. To remove the beating of a fan from above our heads or the ticking of time in our ears, helps us to float. And there, suspended harmoniously, we can exist in tune with ourselves.' I slam the notebook shut and turn to Chris. 'What do you think?'

He looks at me with a puzzled expression. 'Eh, wow, that was pretty good. I like the way you combine the words fan and feet and loneliness together.'

'Is it shit?'

We both burst out laughing.

Suddenly, an animal somewhere in the darkness produces a loud elongated "BAA!"

'What the hell was that?'

'Not sure. Sounded so close.'

With merriment quickly replaced by a sense of fear and freshness, we put on all of the clothes in our small rucksacks and sit with our backs to the tree. We continue to drink wine in the light of my phone until the battery begins to flash red. Using bursts from a clipper lighter to keep an eye on shapes moving in the darkness, we devour a host of snacks before bedding down on the hard earth beneath our foil survival blankets, a bargain at 99 cents.

* * *

I awake to the sound of Si munching on a cereal bar. He tilts his face towards the sun and absorbs its welcoming rays.

I kick away the thin foil blanket that is wet with condensation. 'Traumatic or what!'

Si nods. 'I've never been so cold. I shivered to sleep.'

'What was that screaming?'

'Sheep giving birth or calves being born. Pure horror.'

I wander down to the edge of the lake. 'The mist looks like a steaming kettle. I could murder a coffee.'

Splashing our tired faces in the lake, we return to the trail and pass a field of newborn calves, tiny as lambs. A cheeky chappy buckaroos towards us. His exhausted mother watches on. Si tuts at the infant's youthful enthusiasm.

A short way on, we stumble across a guy with long hair and glasses hiding behind a bush. He carries an enormous rucksack on his shoulders, which dwarfs the tiny ukulele in his hands. We discover Markus is from Zwolle in the Netherlands. He plans to walk the entire 741km from Mérida all the way to Santiago de Compostela in the north of Spain.

Markus finds it hilarious that we are walking in the wrong direction. 'The whole idea of the Camino is to make a pilgrimage to the shrine of Saint James. It is a spiritual path.'

'Is walking in reverse considered bad luck?' Si asks.

'I do not believe so,' Markus replies, strumming his little ukulele. He proceeds to sniff laugh, revealing an essence of madness.

'I hope it doesn't appear disrespectful or symbolise the path of the devil.'

Markus drops his smile and casts us both a look of disdain. Strangely offended, he marches away.

Diving inside a Repsol fuel station near to the town of Alcuéscar, we seize the opportunity to grab a few supplies. We find shade and build a mega sandwich. Si unravels a block of locally produced sheep cheese, and we both gasp and blink as the pungent fumes drift up our nostrils. Despite an odour akin to the putrid smell of old socks, we break the cheese into the bread and feast like wolves. Powered by dairy and plastered in sun cream, we hike towards the never-ending horizon. With sweat evaporating from our skin faster than we can perspire, we make our way towards the Cornalvo Natural Park. The trail winds across a dry landscape, and we pause in the shade beneath a lone holm oak tree. A couple of hikers slide into view. A bubbly woman from Bristol called Fiona quizzes us about our shopping bags, and asks where we found the Spa supermarket. She seems amused when I reveal it is over thirty-five kilometres away in Cáceres.

'You've carried your shopping all of that way?'

'We're not very good at travel,' Si beams.

'You need bigger rucksacks.'

The other hiker is Kathleen from Brisbane in Australia. I am fascinated to learn she has walked here from Granada.

'We're on the run from a very annoying French couple,' Fiona laughs breathlessly. 'We set off before sunrise to get ahead of them. Nothing worse than getting stuck with irritating pilgrims the entire walk. Believe me, it can make even the most religious soul have the darkest of thoughts. Hey, I don't suppose a guy with a ukulele passed you earlier?'

'Markus?'

'Yes, that's him. We met in Seville. Both his parents were tragically killed in a car accident shortly before Christmas. Bit worried about him, really.'

'Poor Markus. He did seem a little strange.'

'You meet all kinds of folk walking the Camino. I'm recently divorced and suffer from depression and Kathleen is a cancer survivor. What happened to you guys?'

Si frowns. 'What'd you mean?'

The women burst out laughing.

Kathleen's nostrils begin to flex. 'What's that disgusting smell?'

'Oh, that's the sheep cheese we bought. I think it might be on the turn.' I whip the cheese out of the shopping bag and wave it in the air.

Fiona squeals and leaps back.

'Strong cheese made by people from a tough land,' Si laughs.

Fiona pinches her nose. 'You can say that again.'

'Would you like to try some?'

'No, thanks!'

Fiona glances at her watch. 'Crikey, time is running. We need to keep ahead of the French. You're welcome to join us if you like.'

'Love to, but we're actually walking in the opposite direction.'

Kathleen looks aghast. 'You're crazy, Simon, it's the burning midday heat. The standard advice is to tackle this section early in the morning when it's cooler.'

Fiona's laugh is infectious. 'My goodness, you boys really aren't very good at travel. Be careful, ok. Only last year a tourist died out here.'

'Died?'

'Yes, there is very little shade and nothing along this stretch for many kilometres. It happened in the month of august when it's blazing hot.'

Persuading ourselves that four litres of water should be enough to survive this treacherous section of the trail, Si leads the way into the searing heat. At the heart of the Cornalvo Natural Park, we soon begin to see large granite boulders scattered across a landscape where wild cats roam. A honey buzzard soars effortlessly on the warm thermals, in a region of Spain that is home to a variety of birds of prey including the griffon vulture. After a few kilometres, we stop by a tree that has been charred by a lightning strike. It is completely hollow in the middle, and Si insists I take a photo of him with his head peering out through the hole.

'Keep the comedy!' he sings, sweat streaming down his shiny red face.

Struggling in the heat along the asphalt trail, sharp stones press painfully against my blisters. With t-shirts wrapped around our heads and our water supply dangerously low, after four long hours we reach a main road. We see a sign for Aljucén, and battle the last kilometre uphill to the centre of the village. With not a soul around and the bar closed, we are relieved to find a drinking fountain. Collapsing onto a park bench I attend to my wounds. Si's feet are so swollen his trainers have split down both sides. In the hope of cooling himself down, he twists a tap attached to a garden hose and boiling hot water that has heated up in the yellow rubber pipe blasts him in the face. I shake my head despairingly as he leaps around and curses the heavens. We push on to the tiny settlement of El Carrascalejo.

A woman walking her two little dogs suddenly appears. 'Hola, you are needing help?' she asks.

It occurs to me that we may look in need of urgent medical attention.

I force a smile. 'No, gracias, thank you. You are very kind.'

'My friend, she has a hostel. You need a hostel?'

'No, it's ok. We are on a journey to Mérida.'

She laughs. 'Walking to Mérida? *Esta noche*? No, no, no, it is very far. You want taxi? My uncle drives taxi.'

'We're saved!' Si sings.

'No way, hippie boy, we must stay focused and true to

our mission.'

His bottom lip begins to quiver. 'But…we slept under a tree.'

'We're not quitting now, goddammit!' I yell. 'Up on your feet, soldier! As the poet Maya Angelou once said, "You will face many defeats in life, but never let yourself be defeated."'

Si mutely nods in acceptance and flips on his shades. With hands on hips the Spanish woman looks bemused as we hobble away.

* * *

With the kilometres falling steadily in time with the setting sun, we repress any pain we feel and stride forth to the horizon. Chris hauls his aching bones over a wooden gate into a cattle field. Either hardened by our walk, or viewing death as welcome respite from the pain that burns in our joints, we feel strangely unafraid of a chance encounter with a fighting bull.

On the rural periphery of Mérida, Lake Proserpina appears magically in view. Through blurred vision we look in awe at the shimmering oasis. We begin to see groups of people out for an evening stroll. A father and son feed ducks on a sandy beach. We pass a bustling waterside café with a sun terrace, the glitzy lights reflect in the water. Travelling at a snail's pace, we limp along a sand covered trail that feels like walking over silk in comparison to the stony track we have endured for the best part of seventy kilometres. We pass fishermen, loving couples and excited children as we struggle over to the head of a stone dam built by the Romans. I collapse on top of a wall as the sun dips behind the trees. Madness spills out of me in a crazed laugh. Chris sits hunched over in complete silence and looks vacantly down at his worn trainers. I can now understand Markus' erratic change in behaviour, insanely strumming a ukulele one minute to suddenly being offended to the core by Chris's mention of the devil.

'I hate to admit failure, Si, but turn me over I'm done.'

'My dogs quit barking over an hour ago. I think they may be dead.'

'The historic centre of Mérida is still five kilometres away.'

I glance over my shoulder. 'We're definitely getting the bus.'

Chris struggles over to a brand new bus stop at the start of a long straight highway. 'This road leads directly to the city of Mérida. We are home and dry, amigo.'

We wait patiently for a bus that never arrives. Inevitable darkness falls quickly all around us. Surprised to discover hidden power, which in our time of crisis rises to the surface like a phoenix from the flames, we muster up the strength to walk. Battling along the dimly-lit Autovía Ruta de la Plata in the dead of night, we are chased by a savage dog. Hurling it the remains of the cheese, we stumble, curse and fight towards the peak of an unreasonably steep hill. Arriving at the top, we look in wonder high over the brightly lit industrial suburbs of Mérida. The last stretch of the hike is more physically challenging than my brain will ever care to remember. We make an agreement that never will we walk anywhere ever again, ever! Chris begins to sing "Eye of the Tiger", an effective motivational technique that in my moment of despair drives me on. Blinded by speeding metal monsters with eyes of fire, we sprint for our lives across an enormous traffic circle. Gaining a sense of the terror of the world of the human, we feel closer to the wild creatures living in the peaceful backcountry of the Extremadura. One of Chris's shopping bags splits open and a cereal bar, a bottle of water and an apple bounce across the road. He grabs what he can, but the apple escapes. We watch helplessly as it rolls down the hill and disappears into the darkness. Warehouses and factories on the outskirts of the city have the appearance of extra-terrestrial structures of unnatural scale. We emerge from a graffiti covered railway bridge in the heart of Mérida's old town, home to the most impressive Roman ruins in all of Spain. Hobbling through the Trajan Arch, we find ourselves in López de Ayala Park. Chris spots a blue neon sign with "Hotel Rambla Emerita" positioned above a row of flags. Staggering like the war wounded towards the entrance, we fall into the hotel lobby and drag ourselves over to the smartly dressed woman standing behind the reception desk.

Mustering up all of the remaining strength in his body, Chris manages to produce a smile and performs scissor fingers. '*Caminado. Mucha distancia*!'

'*Claro*,' she nods, seeming amused.

Much to our relief, the hard faced woman treats us with great care and offers us a room at a very reasonable price. Shuffling over to the elevator, we hunt for 412 and fight with the lock before collapsing onto our beds. Wrestling frantically with his socks, Chris kicks over the bedside lamp. It crashes to the floor and the light cuts out. The last sound I hear as I spiral into the darkness are his whimpering cries and the words "table broken".

A Boat, a Goat & Three Chickens

I walk hurriedly through a bustling market, yellow, orange, pink and blue saris glow bright against the crumbling brick walls. A bony cow munches on newspaper outside a row of shops selling pretty much everything you can imagine from glass bangles, incense and sunglasses, to Bollywood movies and jeans. Rickshaws, cars, horses and carts and motorbikes speed past on a never-ending conveyor belt of madness. You need eyes in the back of your head and a sixth sense to dodge the traffic, the hawkers, the cattle and the crowds.

'*Kya haal hai*!' Si beams, waving me over to a chai stand.

'Where's Darell?'

'Quick haircut. Time to hit the highway or, in this case, the waterway!'

'Why so early?'

'To find a boat. To row to Varanasi.'

We bundle into an auto rickshaw and travel at lightning speed across Allahabad to the Yamuna River and the towering Yamuna Bridge, with its cable-stayed four lane road stretching into the hazy distance. On the banks of the river we look down at dozens of wooden boats at the foot of a steep bank. A guy wearing a red sweater introduces himself as Arnav. He looks surprised when Si asks him if he has a boat for sale.

'You want to buy a boat?'

'We sure do.'

Arnav beams a big smile. 'Yes, yes, please follow me.'

At the river's edge we are shown a four metre long wooden rowing boat. Arnav invites us to hop aboard. A makeshift tarpaulin roof shields us from the burning sun and a green flag dances vigorously from the stern.

'How much?' I ask.

Arnav dives into conversation with a group of men that have crowded around the boat. He then fires a random figure of 28,000 rupees. Racking our brains we quickly work out the exchange rate. We attempt to barter him down, but Arnav shakes his head and holds his price.

'Four hundred dollars,' Darell laughs. 'Not bad for a whole boat.'

Si nods his head in agreement. 'It's a bargain and we can sell it on when we reach Varanasi. What do you think, Chris?'

'How far is Varanasi from here?'

'One hundred and fifty kilometres.'

'Downstream?'

'Yep, once we're in the flow of the river it should be plain sailing all of the way.'

'Ok, let's do it before we lose our nerve.'

Handing over the cash, we ask Arnav for a receipt as proof of purchase along with his contact details and a mobile number. He fishes a scrap of paper out of his back pocket and reluctantly carries out our request. With the paperwork complete, we flag down a cycle rickshaw to take us to the livestock market. We are swiftly delivered to an old brick building, where a pot-bellied gentleman is standing in the doorway with bloodstained hands. Traumatized by the horrors of the slaughter house, we emerge with a cross-eyed goat on a rope. We name him Bruce. Si returns from a nearby market stall with three chickens. Hurrying back to the river, we load our supplies onto the boat and take a moment to familiarize ourselves with the oars. It turns out Darell was a member of the Sea Cadets when he was a teenager, so he has some knowledge of sailing and Si claims to know how to tie a reef knot. Sadly, my own personal experience of boating is limited to a sunny afternoon on a lake in Berlin drinking beer in an inflatable rubber dinghy.

* * *

'Farewell me landlubbers!' Chris hollers, waving to Arnav and a crowd of amused spectators.

Darell seizes the oars with the enthusiasm of a Viking warrior aboard a dragonship, and sets to work at propelling us through the water. Struggling to manoeuvre the large rowing boat in a straight line, we swap over on the approach to the Yamuna Bridge. We laugh hysterically as we spin around in a circle.

'More power on the right side,' Chris commands from the bow.

'The oars are too heavy!' I yell, narrowly avoiding a head-on collision with one of the enormous concrete pillars.

Darell squeezes next to me and we attempt to row side by side.

'Should be easier once we reach the Ganges,' Chris beams, using a plank of wood to paddle from the bow.

Bruce begins to bleat and stomp his little hooves, he then sneezes. He appears to have a cold. The three white chickens flap frantically around our feet exploding sporadically in bursts of feathers.

'Try to keep straight! You're drifting away from the bank.'

We approach the famous Triveni Sangam, the confluence of the Yamuna, the Ganges and a third river, which only exists in a metaphysical form. This location is considered by Hindus to be one of the most sacred pilgrimage sites on the Indian subcontinent.

Chris shields his eyes from the sun. 'Not much further and we meet the Ganges. Row, men, row!'

Overcoming the force of the current, we find we are able to manoeuvre the boat with ease. We release our oars and collapse back in exhaustion. Black smoke from fires and the metronome clang of bells drifts across the water from the crowded north bank. We look in awe at the spectacle of thousands of pilgrims bathing in the water, during an annual fair known as the Magh Mela. Held on the banks of the River Ganges for over 2,000 years, the alignment of stars dictates six specific days when Hindus can wash away their sins, freeing themselves from the cycle of death and rebirth. On a scale of epic proportions, the festival reaches its peak every twelve years when the Kumbh Mela is held drawing crowds in excess of 30 million people. We float in the confluence of the Yamuna and the Ganges where the waters of the two mighty rivers merge. Enjoying a moment of tranquillity, we invite Bruce and the chickens for a picnic. Chris pours water into clay chai cups and sprinkles rice and cabbage leaves on the floor. The chickens dart paranoid glances at one another. The boat turns gently around, and we count a dozen more rowing boats identical to ours overflowing with groups of

Indian pilgrims enjoying the festivities. A hundred metres away a woman makes the offering of a *deepak*, a small banana leaf boat containing yellow and red flowers and an oil lamp. It bobs gently up and down on the surface of the water. Her family and the boatman look with curiosity at the strange Westerners snacking on samosas, who are accompanied by a goat and three chickens.

Wrapping t-shirts around my hands, I grab the oars and paddle slowly along the shoreline. On the periphery of a vast floodplain that is covered by an ocean of large canvas tents, thousands of pilgrims walk in a line to the bathing areas across a network of floating pontoons. The colour of the water is muddy orange where the sacred rivers meet. Drifting slowly on the current away from the crowds and the mayhem of the festival, we begin to pick up speed. It becomes clear our job now is less about paddling and more about steering. Chris leaps into action as navigator, while Darell and I attempt to use the oars to turn our trusty vessel. Approaching what appears to be an old wooden fence submerged in the water, we aim for a gap and are thrust forward over minor rapids. A large cargo barge sweeps past generating a series of waves that cause the boat to rock violently from side to side. Bruce begins to bleat once more and the chickens release more bursts of panic. Without warning a dolphin suddenly arches out of the water beside the boat, its grey body glistens in the sunlight. Before travelling to India, I had read about blind river dolphins living in the heavily polluted waters of the Ganges, but I never imagined we would actually see one. An incredible 40% of India's human population live along the Ganges, which is a mind boggling 500 million people. The result is a river overflowing with untreated sewage and industrial waste. Not exactly a paradise habitat for the 1,500 dolphins who call this river home.

* * *

As the city of Allahabad and the magnificent spectacle of the Magh Mela slide out of view, it grows eerily quiet. We rest for a moment and attend to our bleeding hands that have been completely rubbed raw. I sit in silence and contemplate our situation. The thought of embarking on a river journey without a detailed map begins to seem crazy. What were we thinking? For all we know we could be heading straight towards dangerous rapids, whirlpools or waterfalls where crocodiles, snakes and all manner of monsters lie in wait. We pass a small sandbank island that is occupied by a flock of hungry vultures picking at the carcass of a water buffalo. I suddenly notice a strange looking object floating towards us. Si uses his paddle to draw it closer. Rocking in the current, the black object flips over onto its side and we look in horror at the disturbing sight of the bloated and decomposing body of a young boy. The three of us recoil in fright and collapse back into the boat. The boy's mouth is wide open in an apparent scream, and there are two gaping black holes where his eyes used to be. The corpse floats alongside the rowing boat, close enough to touch. In an attempt to escape the living horror movie playing out in front of us, we all begin churn water. Bruce wanders between Si's feet causing him to stumble. Inching closer and closer towards the shallow river bank, Si and Darell lean over the port side and use their paddles to push away. With their arms at full stretch, I grab hold of their t-shirts in a bid to prevent them both toppling overboard.

Back on course and with slight distance between us and the corpse, Si pants breathlessly. 'Do you think we should call the police?'

'The police?'

'Yes, there's a dead body in the water! The poor kid could have been murdered.'

'The river is full of corpses. You didn't know?'

'No, I didn't funnily enough. I thought Hindu's cremated their dead.'

'Funeral pyres cost money. Not everyone can afford the wood. Unmarried women and children are often buried in shallow graves along the riverbank. When water levels rise in the monsoon the bodies get washed into the river.'

Si leaps to his feet. 'Hey, I can see a sandbank below the surface of the water.'

Darell snatches a paddle and joins Si at the back of the boat.

'Which way, Chris, which way?'

Darell's eyes widen. 'Getting seriously shallow this side.'

'I'm not sure! More to the right.'

The further we move away from the bank the faster the flow of the water. Picking up speed, we struggle to steer in a straight line and are thrust towards a second sandbank. There is nothing we can do apart from hold on. The boat runs aground with significant force and we are flung violently forward. A group of kids run over. They howl and cry out as they surround the boat. The noise is deafening. Thin and black from the sun, the kids fire questions at us in Hindi. It is quite possible we are the first Europeans they have ever seen. With big smiles, they appear friendly and I begin to feel more relaxed. Si speaks to them in a gentle, but authoritative manner and we learn these sand islands are known as *chars*. Si encourages the kids to help us rock the boat free. All is going brilliantly until a dishevelled Indian guy wearing a torn blanket appears. He stares at me with the most haunting bloodshot eyes. Muttering to himself, he looks over at a group of men squatting outside a makeshift shelter. They rise to their feet. I instinctively sense they are not about to offer us a helping hand. Wearing baggy suit trousers that hang from his bony hips, the guy enters the water and shouts at the kids. Happy screams of excitement are replaced by deafening silence. I curse at our arrogance and naivety for thinking we could navigate this river without a guide. I turn to Bruce for help, but he just looks up at me with big watery eyes and floppy ears. He sneezes and returns to eating the boat.

'*Danikka*! *Danikka*!' The guy shouts. His face is drawn and weather-beaten and he appears to be drunk or high on drugs. He then turns to Si. '*Danikka*! *Danikka*!'

Growing agitated, he continues to scream at the top of his voice. He pounds the boat with a clenched fist and grinds his rotten teeth. This guy is completely insane. I feel immediately trapped and incredibly vulnerable. My mind races. He doesn't appear to have a weapon, so maybe we can knock him to the ground. The three of us could easily restrain him. Then I think of the potentially devastating consequences of trying to be the hero, with no clear indication of how his buddies on the bank may respond. The thought of being murdered for odd socks, unwashed underpants and a t-shirt with a faded picture of Gandhi emblazoned across the front, suddenly seems unwise. The guy orders one of the older boys to fetch something from the river bank. The kid appears reluctant at first, but fearful of what might happen if he disobeys he eventually follows his orders. Feeling more powerful, the savage continues to rant. He turns his attention to Darell and mimes cutting his throat. He then points at the Ganges and impersonates a dead body floating in the water, as if to suggest that if we do not follow his instructions this is how we will end up. His chapped lips are seeping blood and a string of red saliva hangs from the corner of his mouth. There is no doubt in my mind that this rotten specimen of a human being would kill and not feel any remorse. We are not from around here and no matter how sick in the head this guy may be, this is his tribe, his world and his stretch of the river. Expressing deep irritation, there is nothing more we can do apart from accept the fact that we are being robbed and hand over what little we have. I jab my fingers into my pockets and whip out a five-hundred rupee note, less than ten US dollars. He snatches it out of my hand and then points at Darell and Si. They too empty their wallets and hand over their cash. The psychopath mutters something before wading off through the water. Not wanting to outstay our welcome, Darell springs overboard into the heavily polluted water and with help from the kids they free the heavy wooden boat from the sandbank.

* * *

Chris thrusts his paddle into the water and pushes off the riverbed with all of his might. In a bid to reach deeper water, we wage war against the fierce current and together haul the rowing boat upstream. I breathe through my nostrils and try to block out the thought of what horrors lie beneath the surface. Once the river water reaches our chests we struggle aboard. In agreement that we need to return upriver to the sanctuary and relative safety of the outer suburbs of the city before nightfall, we paddle with all of the remaining strength in our bodies. After a few minutes, my hands are literally bleeding from where the paddles have rubbed away the skin. With the sunset rapidly approaching, we begin to feel trapped out here on the Ganges. Soon it will be dark. At the point where we begin to feel absolute despair, I suddenly spot a barge making its way upriver.

'We're saved!' Chris sings.

We all punch the air and cheer as the barge draws to a halt a short way downstream. Allowing ourselves to drift on the current at a steady angle, we grip the bloated wooden hull with flat palms. Hollering at the top of our voices, a face suddenly peers over the side. We plead for the man's help, but rather than welcoming us aboard with a giant smile, he looks deeply annoyed and disappears out of sight.

'Where's he gone?' Chris yells, the strain starting to show.

'Maybe he's not legally permitted to help us.'

'Why not?'

'I don't know. Insurance reasons?'

'Insurance reasons? Si, we're on a boat in the middle of the Ganges. First world bullshit does not apply here.'

'What would Bollywood superstar Shahrukh Khan do in this situation?'

'Probably call his agent.'

At that precise moment, a rope falls from the sky. The captain of the ship, a tough guy wearing a lungi as a turban, leads the rowing boat to the rear of the barge. We scramble onto the bank. Invited aboard we are met by a Government worker who has chartered the vessel. He reveals he is using sonar to measure the depth of the river. Agreeing to tow us to a port ten kilometres down river, we travel the last stretch of our Ganges river journey by barge. We stand with Rishu and watch a dramatic sunset paint orange flames across the sky. The captain of the barge calls down to us from the wheelhouse and we see three

97

silhouetted dolphins arch out of the water.

In the still of night, we draw up alongside a cluster of makeshift huts. A group of men are sitting around a roaring fire. Rishu offers us a ride into town.

'What about Bruce and the chickens?' Chris asks.

'Isn't the boat our main concern right now?'

'We could call Arnav?' Darell suggests.

Rishu glances at his watch. 'My wife. My son. They are waiting for me in the home.'

'Yes, of course. Sorry, Rishu.' I turn to Chris and Darell. 'I kind of just want to get out of here.'

'It's been a pretty mad adventure,' Darell laughs. 'We got away with it.'

'Do you want the boat, Rishu?' I smile. 'Call it a gift for rescuing us.'

He wisely declines, which isn't surprising when you consider the wild manner in which we met. Chris asks Rishu if the captain may be interested in taking it off our hands. After all, he clearly likes boats.

Rishu responds with a mute shrug. He glances at the group of guys sitting around the fire. 'These local fishermen, they are very poor. They live here on the Ganges. You can leave the boat with them if you wish.'

Happy to give something back to the people in this region, who are clearly struggling for survival on the shores of one of Earth's most polluted rivers, we retrieve our small backpacks and leave everything else behind. Chris lifts Bruce out of the boat and sets him free along with the chickens. In a short space of time these charismatic creatures have crossed the invisible boundary of food and become our friends.

We arrive at the transport terminal in the dead of night, it's buzzing with religious pilgrims. People sleep on blankets on the ground as charcoal smoke from food stalls merges with burning incense and the smell of spice. A group of holy men chant mantras inside a nearby temple, the sound of bells competing with car horns in the street outside. Rishu kindly invites us for chai and insists we call him if we have any further problems whilst travelling in India. He explains that to attempt our journey without an experienced guide or armed security was a huge risk. Feeling foolish and humbled by his kindness, we jump aboard a bus bound for Varanasi. Feeling relieved to be back in civilization, I watch the chaos of India streaming past my window. Our quest to row the Ganges has been a complete and utter disaster. It was an adventure that spiralled out of control. With new appreciation for life and death, we have been forced to learn a valuable lesson; a journey into unknown waters requires preparation, knowledge and guidance and survival in the face of danger demands calm and the company of good friends.

Date with the Devil

High over the terracotta rooftops we look in awe at the mesmerising red mountain that looms over Potosi.

'Cerro Rico means Rich Mountain,' Maria, a student of tourism, beams. 'It is one of the largest silver mines in the world.'

Si pokes his head around a large cast iron bell. 'We have to go inside!'

'Hate to focus on the negatives, buddy, but what happens if we get blown apart by dynamite, or crushed to death by a collapsing mine shaft. Not to mention the threat of suffocation and slow death by poisonous gases?'

Maria snaps a quick selfie. 'My cousin, he was working inside Cerro Rico. He told me it is really like hell.'

After nearly two weeks on the road with Si and fellow travelling companion Darell, we have arrived in a Bolivian Andean settlement at a dizzying elevation of over 4,000 metres. Maria points out numerous church spires, and reveals there are a total of twenty-two parish or monastic churches in a city that was once a centre of spectacular wealth. Three hundred years ago, Potosi had an incredibly large population similar to London during the same era. The Spanish gave South America Jesus, railways and modern government, but it stole from the mines and left very little behind.

Maria leads us down to the enormous central nave of the cathedral. It is built in baroque and neoclassical colonial styles with towering pillars painted aqua blue and gold. She unwisely invites the talentless trio to play the organ that includes a row of brass pipes resembling rockets aimed at the heavens. Darell and Si fill the mighty Basilica of Our Lady of Peace with the organ classic "Chopsticks", closely followed by a rendition of "Twinkle, Twinkle, Little Star".

Bidding Maria farewell, we jump aboard a colectivo bound for the mine. Si fires questions at our fellow passenger Claus, a German tourist in his early sixties, who has a touch of the Clint Eastwood about him.

'I have spent the past six months driving the Pan-American Highway,' he proudly informs us. I shipped my vehicle to the east of Canada, so I have travelled a very long way.'

'See any bears?'

'Oh, ja, many.' Claus falls silent and glances down at his phone. 'My mother was taken to hospital last night. She has been unwell for some days now.'

'Not easy when you're so far away from home.'

'I have been looking at flights, but I do not want to leave my bitch.'

'Your bitch?'

'Ja, my dog. I found her injured on the road in Colombia.'

'I'm sure your mum will be ok.'

'My wife is taking care of her. She was not well before I left Munich six months ago, but I am not so young myself. I have wanted to make this trip for many years.'

Our conversation is cut short when the colectivo grinds

to a sudden halt. The sliding door is flung open and a stern-faced young woman peers inside. She turns to the pale looking guy standing beside her. 'Why are there tourists here?'

He shrugs his shoulders.

'You are geologists?' she snaps.

'No, we're…' I glance at Si, Darell and Claus. '…aging backpackers.'

Our little group gathers around a store that spills out onto the sidewalk from a two storey breezeblock building. Soledad, our tour leader, addresses us with an air of confidence. She stands with her shoulders and head back, and describes a typical day in the life of a Potosi miner. Most mornings, the workers visit a local store on this street and stock up with supplies before making the journey up the mountain. Soledad takes a large pinch of green leaves balanced on a set of antique scales.

'Coca,' she nods firmly.

She then stuffs the dry leaves into the left side of her mouth, and takes a bite out of a piece of black chalk-like substance.

'Alkaline activator,' she mumbles, handing it to Darell. 'You take.'

Darell seizes the moment and stuffs a clump of leaves into his mouth. Soledad points at the activator and he gingerly takes a bite. Si is up next and I join in close behind in third place. Claus and the Italian couple, Stefano and Luna, appear reluctant.

'Panda food,' I smile, my cheek bulging with leaves.

Si laughs uncontrollably, green leaves stuck between his teeth. 'The activator, it tastes minty.'

Soledad explains that the coca leaves give energy and repress appetite, while helping to reduce the symptoms of altitude sickness. Within a few minutes of chewing the leaves, our cheeks and throats begin to feel numb. Next on the Bolivian miner's breakfast menu is a local beverage, with an eye-watering alcohol volume of 96%. Soledad cracks open a small plastic bottle of Ceibo, a brand of white spirit made from sugar cane that the local Aymara call *cocoroco*. Soledad takes a swig before passing it around. Claus joins in the fun. The warm sensation of the potent alcohol burns through our digestive systems and, combined with the euphoric effects of the coca leaves, I begin to appreciate why a Bolivian miner (for good or bad) may choose to utilise these substances. With a noticeable increase in heart rate, I curiously scan the products for sale at the store; miner's helmets, bright blue rope and cowboy-style bandanas for covering your nose and mouth from the dust. I consider buying a toilet roll that Si jokes would be useful for when we shit ourselves.

Redirecting my focus, Soledad points at me with a baton of rolled up white paper that has a lime green fuse hanging out of the end.

'*¿Que es esto?*' she asks.

We all look puzzled.

'Dynamite!' she replies.

Fascinated to learn that here in Potosi it is legal to buy and sell explosives in local stores, I require no further persuasion and invest in the roll of toilet paper.

* * *

Chris emerges from a miner's cottage wearing mustard overalls, black rubber boots and an orange helmet. With heavy-duty batteries strapped around our waists to power our headlamps I hold onto my belt, which feels like a gun holster. Soledad treats Stefano roughly, and saddles him with the burden of carrying four large bottles of a syrupy

103

orange drink in a hessian sack. I get the impression the Italian couple had insisted on making some kind of extreme tour. On route to the mine I discover that in addition to Spanish Soledad also speaks Aymara, one of only a handful of Native American languages with over one million speakers. Behind a tough exterior lies a kind woman who is the mother of a teenage daughter. Soledad started as a guide when she was twenty four. A proud member of the mining community, her grandfather worked in the cavernous depths of Cerro Rico along with many other family members, who continue to carve a living from the mountain to this very day.

Zigzagging to the top of the towering pyramid of red rock, we pass a black marble statue. The sculpture depicts a strong miner on a crucifix who is pointing at the sky. He is accompanied by a group of fellow miners with clenched fists. Squeezed between Chris and the driver, Soledad points a purple manicured nail at a two-storey building with "Co-operativa Minera" emblazoned across the front. The date March 27th, 1988, is printed below in block capitals. The cooperatives in Potosi were formed during a painful period of relocation and job losses of around 25,000 state workers. Many miners suddenly found themselves without employment, so they organized themselves into mining cooperatives in order to generate their own economic resources. Soledad started working as a guide during this period when mineral prices were low and jobs scarce. Two female labourers, wearing layered skirts worn traditionally by the Andean people of this region, stand by a wheelbarrow at the foot of a row of large concrete chutes. They wait patiently for a group of men to load a truck. Brown wide-brimmed sombreros shield their faces from the sun, and their hair is tied neatly back in two long braids. I ask Soledad if she also wears traditional clothes. She cracks a smile. For the mine she feels more comfortable wearing jeans, t-shirt and a fleece. Chris shows Soledad photographs on his camera of fashionable women in La Paz, known as *cholitas*, wearing bowler hats balanced at impossible angles on top of their heads. She reveals the hats are known locally as *borsalino*. The bowler grew in popularity with the local Andean people in the late 1800s, during a period when the windproof hat was worn by British railway workers and cowboys in the American West. The driver sounds the horn. Outside a cluster of small brick buildings, we pass half a dozen men wearing baseball caps and tracksuit tops. From our mountain perch, we look down over Potosi eight-hundred metres into the valley below. Chris and Darell examine a rusty mining wagon that we assume is a relic of the past. I look in astonishment when a group of men begin positioning it on the tracks at the entrance to the mine. Once Soledad has the all clear from the miners, she makes sure we are prepared for our expedition into this hostile environment. We check our headlamps are working. Darell suddenly realises he has left his facemask at the miner's cottage. The impatient Italian couple roll their eyes. Unfazed, he demonstrates that by using the sleeve of his jumper to cover his nose and mouth everything is cool. With Soledad's cheek bulging with coca leaves she leads us bravely into the darkness.

'Say goodbye to the sunlight,' Chris sings, as we splash through puddles of rainwater in our rubber boots.

I glance over my shoulder at frequent intervals and watch the tunnel entrance shrink to a small circle of light. In the dark recesses of Cerro Rico, Soledad warns us to mind our heads as we prepare to enter a much smaller tunnel made from blocks of stone. I immediately notice the rock at the entrance is covered in what appears to be red paint.

Chris turns sharply in my direction, blinding me with his headlamp. 'It looks like someone has been murdered!'

Luna steps forward. 'No, no, it is not blood at all. I believe gases in the mine have turned the stone crimson.'

Claus speaks to Soledad in Spanish. '*Sangre de llama*?'

She nods.

'Ja, so, it is actually the blood of a llama.'

'How did it get there?' Chris asks.

'It is a very ancient Andean ritual,' Claus replies. 'The local people of Potosi sacrifice a llama and smear its blood on the entrance to the mines.'

Keen to get moving, Soledad waves us on. Chris smacks his helmet on a low beam. Our combined laughter echoes through the tunnel. Struggling to walk in a hunched position for long, I join him in beating my head against a protruding rock with such force it momentarily causes my headlamp to cut out. Grit falls all around me. We pause briefly to look at mineral deposits that are yellow and turquoise blue, like the plumage of a macaw. Soledad explains that in addition to silver the mountain was also mined in the 12th century for tin and zinc, together with by-product copper and lead. I ask Soledad if she ever wonders why tourists come here. She appears amused by my question, and believes people travel to the mines to de-stress and value what they have. De-stress? Breathing in a lungful of foul smelling air, my chest begins to feel unusually tight. Worryingly, Chris also begins to look strained. Deep in concentration, we stumble in silence through the darkness along a network of never-ending tunnels. The line comes to a sudden and abrupt halt. I feel claustrophobic and focus on my breathing. I wrestle negativity and try to block out the thought that we are deep inside this labyrinth of rock, with no emergency oxygen or quick escape route out of here. Claus is noticeably silent. The line begins to move again. Up ahead I see Stefano squeeze into a narrow hole and climb vertically upwards. Luna is next, and we all follow one another driven by the fear of being left behind. Luna calls down to us and signals a spiral up head. It appears we have to turn up and back on ourselves in a corkscrew motion. Scrambling in our rubber boots, a cloud of dust fills the small tunnel. Darell covers his mouth and nose with his sleeve. I become disorientated and, for a frightening few seconds, I no longer have any idea which way is up and which way is down.

* * *

Soledad leads us to a cavern that is curiously occupied by a red statue of the devil. She refers to the sculpture as El Tio (the Uncle), and wedges a lit cigarette between the horned creature's lips. Wrestling to untangle himself from the cable connecting the battery around his waist to his helmet, Si accidentally brushes his elbow against El Tio's huge erect penis. I ask Soledad if the miners worship the devil. She looks slightly miffed, and I get the distinct impression that El Tio is in one way a mascot and a symbol of this hellish environment. The miners routinely give El Tio coca leaves and cigarettes, and ask for his protection in the hostile and dangerous world of the mine. I guess who else would live down here other than the lord of the darkness.

Stefano looks irritated. 'This mountain, it formed a very long time before the evolution of any creatures that would look like this.'

'It's only a bit of fun,' Si muses, his face covered in dust. 'Imagine how terrifying it would have been

107

hundreds of years ago with only flickering candles to light the way. To believe a devil uncle was watching over you may have been quite useful.'

Soledad explains that El Tio offers the miners both protection and destruction, and that they take the practise of giving him cigarettes, coca leaves and alcohol very seriously. If they do not make offerings, they believe he will take matters into his own hands.

Darell balances a second cigarette on El Tio's head. 'I'm taking no chances,' he winks.

Soledad pours a drop of the 96% miner's alcohol onto the ground by El Tio's feet. 'For Pachamama,' she nods, taking a sip. She hands the *cocoroco* to Si.

We are surprised to discover the burning alcohol helps to ease the feeling of tightness in our chests. Soledad explains that often the miner's drink some alcohol to help "clean inside", and that the main reason they perform the *challa* is to honour Pachamama, who they believe embodies the mountains and is responsible for earthquakes. A loud boom shakes the rock beneath us.

Stefano looks around in panic. 'What the hell is this?' he cries, sounding very Italian all of a sudden.

Soledad asks us all to remain calm and explains that a couple of miners are working close by with explosives. We cautiously follow Soledad out of the devil's chamber, and wait while she speaks to two tough mine workers at the far end of the tunnel. With bandanas wrapped around their faces they have the appearance of Wild West bandits. Si asks one of the guys, who is protruding halfway out of a hole in the tunnel floor, why he isn't wearing a protective mask. He seems amused, and we get the impression they regard them as not very cool. The other miner is wearing a Bolivian football shirt and has a playful demeanour. He asks if we can help him find work in our country. We are amazed to discover the two friends have been working together at Cerro Rico for over twenty years. They look surprisingly fit and healthy considering the average lifespan of a career miner in Bolivia is only around forty to fifty years old. I ask if they ever encounter problems with other miners. They explain that helping one another is top priority in an environment fraught with danger. Respect it seems is vital for survival. Kindly demonstrating how to roll a tube of dynamite, they accept a bottle of orange and a bag of coca leaves with gratitude. With the explosives ready to ignite, we wisely leave them to concentrate on their work and hastily race after Soledad who marches away at speed. Nervous laughter echoes through the tunnel at hearing the sound of the exploding dynamite. A second deep rumble reverberates through the mountain.

* * *

Confident to trust our powerful guide, Chris flips his mask over his face and raises his thumbs. With no clear idea how long our journey will last, we make our way deeper and deeper into the mine. We turn a corner and meet two kids pushing a wagon that is heavily loaded with jagged pieces of ore. They are both incredibly short of breath. The younger of the duo looks no older than seventeen. He is wearing a silver shell suit jacket, which gives him the appearance of a spaceman. Glancing over at Chris and Darell wearing their ill-fitting miner's outfits, it occurs to me that we look like a crew of badly cast actors in a low budget Sci-Fi movie. Soledad snaps her fingers at Stefano. He mutters under his breath and hands over a bottle of the well-earned sugary fuel. Chris examines a sparkling chunk of rock in the mining cart, which we learn is not silver at all, but rather some other precious ore.

Encouraging them to return to their work, Soledad instructs us to help push their heavy burden along the track. Our team effort gives them enough momentum to make it around the corner on a steep gradient, and they disappear into the darkness. Incredibly, during the boom times of the mine, the hard work transporting the ore through the tunnels was only carried out by Indian slaves and forced labourers. Approximately 5,100 of the 58,800 miners working at Potosi in the year 1603 were classed as slaves. The others were contractual workers *mingas* (an Inca term), numbering 10,500, in addition to 43,200 free wage earners, all of whom would refuse to do the incredibly hard work being performed over 400 years later by the two young guys we had just met. The mortality rate, however, was far more extreme in the early days of colonial rule. Many workers died from pneumonia partly as a result of appalling living conditions, or from mercury poisoning during the refining process. In addition to Native Americans, African slaves were also used as human mules in Potosi's Mint 'Casa de la Moneda', to replace the animals that kept dying from exhaustion. It was a brutal period in history.

Continuing our great odyssey in the bowels of Cerro Rico, we pause en route to study a small cavern that has been blown out with dynamite to reveal rock that twinkles like diamonds in our headlamps. Soledad explains that this is Fool's silver. Chris snaps a shot of a sign with a drawing of the devil on it. This second shrine is home to a life-size clay statue of El Tio. Luna appears more relaxed and appoints herself the job of educating us about the geology of Cerro Rico. I am fascinated to learn that we are in actual fact hanging out with the devil inside an extinct volcano. The ore deposits that are so highly prized by humans are concentrated in veins that pass through the volcanic dome, reaching from the summit to depths of 1,150 metres.

'This mountain is like beeswax,' explains Luna. 'It's honeycomb inside from overmining.'

Chris glances up at the rocky ceiling. 'We were warned by a traveller from Santiago that we should not visit the mine, because a few years ago a giant sinkhole appeared on top of the mountain.'

Luna tilts back her helmet and fixes Chris with wide eyes. 'Yes, it is true. The summit of the mountain is sinking a few centimetres every year. It is inevitable that someday the mountain will collapse.'

Stefano appears anxious. 'They put cement in the hole, but what can you do about a collapsing mountain?'

'Cerro Rico and Potosi were added to the UNESCO list of endangered sites,' reveals Luna. 'But I cannot imagine they will do anything about it. Fifteen-thousand workers depend on this mine for their livelihood.'

The journey back out of the mountain is tough. Soledad seems concerned about time, and at one point looks slightly panicked by the route she has chosen. If our batteries run out of power, we will be completely swallowed up by Cerro Rico, known for centuries as "the mountain that eats men". Soledad asks Chris to hold onto her arm as she calls down an empty tunnel, her voice echoes in the eerie blackness. Seeming unsure about what work is being carried out in this less visited section of Cerro Rico, I get a sense of how quickly events can spiral out of control. She makes the wise decision to backtrack. Stefano looks broken from carrying the heavy hessian sack. I want to offer to relieve him of his burden, but my breathing still feels laboured. It is survival time. Like *Alice in Wonderland*, we crawl into the rabbit hole one by one and squeeze through the narrow vertical mine shaft that leads to the lower level. The last few hundred metres out of the mine requires enormous stamina. I strike my helmet on a rock so violently the light completely goes out and I am left staggering in the pitch darkness at the back of the pack. Wading through deep water along the main track, we eventually spot a circle of light in the distance. As we march closer I can taste fresh, clean air. Emerging into the blinding sunlight, we are welcomed by a group of miners. They shake our hands with powerful grips, and smile at our confused faces which rapidly explode in expressions of joy.

The atmosphere inside the colectivo is one of great relief as we wind our way back down the mountain to Potosi. Chris asks Soledad if she will continue to work at the mine for many more years. She confesses that when her daughter leaves school she may be curious to try something new. She doesn't mention the dangers of working in the mine and I draw incredible strength from the stoic bravery of the local people, who endure incredibly challenging conditions in order to make a life in the high Andes. Speeding past endless crumbling colonial buildings, relics left behind by the Spanish after the city's wealth declined, I smile at the thought that the true worth of Potosi was never really in the mine. It exists in the hearts of the kind, hardworking people who continue to thrive here in the mountains at the rooftop of the world.

The Frida Kahlo Experience

It is the Easter holidays in Mexico City and the streets of the historic centre are blissfully calm. I first travelled to the land of tequila more than a decade ago with Chris, following a road trip across the United States in a brown van called Hank. We were twenty-five, naive, and mainly on the hunt for the best beaches on the Yucatán Peninsula. The chance to finally see something in this mega metropolis, finds us both champing at the bit. High priority on my list of things to see is La Casa Azul, the house museum where the Mexican painter Frida Kahlo lived with her family for much of her life. With his own personal mission to document the streetlife here, and, of course, seek out the world's best tacos in the land where they originate from, Chris accompanies me on an urban adventure in a city that has a population of over 21 million people.

I had first been introduced to Frida's work many years ago while on assignment in the Argentine Capital of Buenos Aires. My friend Martina was working as a journalist for the Argentinean newspaper *La Nación*, and she had kindly arranged an interview to discuss the release of our third book *Carnival Express*. With work out of the way, Martina suggested we drink coffee at the Museum of Latin American Art. Powered by caffeine, we explored a section of the gallery displaying works of Surrealism. Keen to show me one particular painting, I recall, with striking clarity, a colourful self-portrait of a dark haired, olive skinned Latin woman with a coquettish gaze. What immediately struck me was the strength and individuality of the person looking out from the painting. She wore her hair in a similar style to the indigenous women of Central and South America that we had seen and photographed over the years. Her clothes were equally traditional and colourful, and her eyes framed by a thick black monobrow, that I found at the time slightly shocking and strangely hypnotic. The shadow of fine black hair on her top lip was accentuated by the black fur of the pet monkey in her arms, while the green parrot perched on her shoulder projected a similar exotic sense that this woman belonged to the earth, was natural, uninhibited and very much alive. I was unable to forget this haunting image of Frida Kahlo. To me, she was the absolute personification of Latin America, this single painting combining all the elements that had left an impression on us both during our time traversing this fascinating and culturally inspiring region of the world.

* * *

Outside our crumbling hotel in the gritty backstreets of the centro histórico, I find Si leaning against a lime green VW Beetle. A well-dressed chap skips out of a nearby apartment building and dives behind the wheel. He grinds the worn out gearbox into first and splutters down the potholed road, leaving us both choking on a thick black cloud of exhaust fumes. Manufactured in Mexico since the late 1960s, it's impossible not to smile at seeing these classic cars still in operation as taxi cabs across the city. In the shadow of the enormous Metropolitan Cathedral on the north side of Plaza de la Constitución, we watch with fascination as an Aztec folk healer performs a spiritual cleansing ceremony. The deeply tanned guy is stripped to the waist and wearing a headdress of eagle and exotic birds feathers. Predominantly Mexican tourists and day trippers take turns to be blessed by the barefooted shaman, who burns a variety of herbs in a wooden goblet and circles the smoke around their heads. Si reveals that we are in fact standing at the centre of what was once the former sacred precinct of the Aztec capital of Tenochtitlan. The arrival of the Spanish conquistador Hernán Cortés and his men 500 years ago, triggered the collapse of the Aztec Empire, and marked the beginning of centuries of Spanish colonial rule. The entire sacred site including the great Aztec pyramids of Templo Mayor, were later destroyed by the invaders, and this enormous cathedral and plaza were built in its place. Christianisation of Latin America had begun.

Diving into the subterranean world of the metro, a live band performs for the commuters as we navigate a labyrinth of tunnels and escalators leading to the train platform. Buzzing from the thrill of being in such a vibrant city, Si waves me aboard a train that transports us a few kilometres southeast to the small barrio of Coyoacan. Suffering from a mild tequila hangover, we wander through the tranquil plaza and gorge on delicious tlacoyos; a delicious corn snack that dates back to the Aztec times. We try chicharron (braised pork belly), haba (mashed fava beans), and requesón (a fresh Mexican cheese similar to ricotta). With mouths burning from red salsa, we duck into a nearby saloon bar and wash down our lunch with ice cold bottles of Modelo beer. Shaded tree-lined avenues provide welcome relief from the midday heat, as we pass a row of colonial mansion houses with wrought iron gates. Coyoacan was least affected by the terrible earthquake that struck Mexico City in 1985, and today is an affluent neighbourhood with funky pavement café's on every corner. Walking on a carpet of purple blossom along Calle Londres, we find ourselves standing outside a bright blue house known as La Casa Azul. Entering the museum, our first introduction to Frida's world is the sight of a girl projectile vomiting in front of a portrait of Frida's close friend Agustin Olmedo. The poor girl is ushered away by her angry mother while a member of staff slides into view with a mop. Less familiar with the artist's work than Si, I examine an early painting by Frida Kahlo. It is a family portrait, and I catch myself smiling at how proud she clearly was of her ethnic mix. Si reveals that it was Frida's exotic appearance that had initially struck him about her work, when he had seen her self-portrait in Buenos Aires. Reading about the life of one of Mexico's greatest artists as we drift around the gallery, I am fascinated to learn that Frida's father was born in Pforzheim in Germany to Jewish parents. Her mother's ancestry was a mix of Spanish and Amerindian (the indigenous peoples of the Americas). Frida celebrated her Amerindian roots in her work, and later in her style and dress. Her artist husband Diego Rivera was attracted to the powerful Zapotec women from the region, and she had dresses made in red, green, blue, black and white. Her fashion was far from conventional for the time, and rather amusingly it was apparently not unusual for children in the street to ask her if the circus was in town.

* * *

I stand and stare with morbid fascination at Frida's famous painting 'Henry Ford Hospital', which depicts her tragic miscarriage in 1932. Scanning the room I feel acutely aware that the majority of visitors to the museum appear to be female. The striking image of Frida lying naked and exposed on a hospital bed with masses of blood covering the sheets begins to make me feel slightly uneasy. Various symbols project from her body, her damaged pelvis, her miscarried foetus. Celebrated for the uncompromising depiction of the female experience in her work, I begin to question why I find her paintings so captivating. Then it hits me. It's her rage I like, her screaming pain. Frida's paintings are loud. They would stir emotion in the most glacial of folk. They alarm and they are earth tremblingly dramatic. Sure it's the female experience she's shouting about, but you get a sense she would shout equally loud if she were a man. Entering the next room I view a colourful painting of water melons. One slice of melon has the words "Vive la vida" (Live life) written across it; a haunting phrase that the artist wrote eight days before she died. I feel a rush of positivity in contrast to the scene of tragic loss portrayed in the previous painting. This is, in my opinion, the Frida Kahlo experience. Taking a step back, I bump into Chris. He whispers a quote by Frida plastered across the wall. "Banks of a river don't suffer by letting it flow." Frida was forced to endure great pain both emotionally and physically in her relatively short life. She died aged 47, but in art it seems clear she found a way of managing, expressing and channelling her suffering and anguish in a very positive way. Before arriving at La Casa

Azul, I had been dubious about how I might feel after having a deeper insight into Frida's past, but as we make our way around her home I find myself liking her even more.

Frida had contracted polio at a very young age, causing her considerable discomfort and leaving her with one withered leg shorter than the other. Wearing long, colourful skirts helped her to disguise this, as well as wearing boots with one heel larger than the other. If this were not difficult enough, at the tender age of eighteen, Frida was involved in a catastrophic bus accident. Her horrific injuries included a broken spinal column, collarbone, ribs, pelvis, a leg fractured in eleven places and a crushed and dislocated foot. As a result of her misfortune, she was left bedridden for much of her life and her reproductive capacity compromised due to an iron handrail piercing her abdomen and her uterus. Frida was quoted as saying in the book, *Frida Kahlo* by Andrea Kettenmann, "I paint myself because I am so often alone and because I am the subject I know best."

As we continue to explore the Blue House, I study the black and white prints of Frida on the walls, and begin to feel better acquainted with the woman who had grabbed my attention with such force more than a decade ago. The honesty of her work and passion in her expression seem genuine and refreshingly pure. Frida had married a man twice her age, who she had met whilst still at school. Diego Rivera was a prominent Mexican painter and he was a huge inspiration and love in Frida's life. Chris points out two ceramic clocks standing side by side in the bright colourful dining room. A friendly museum volunteer, with a startling monobrow, tells the story of how Frida had painted the time on the first clock to represent time stopping after discovering her husband

Diego was having an affair with her sister. She painted the time on the second clock, when time began again following their remarriage a year later. Chris leads the way up a staircase and glows beetroot red when he trips over his big banana feet, causing a party of women wearing floral summer dresses to laugh and babble noisily in Spanish. We enter the room where Frida and Diego would paint, and I try to imagine the conversations (and arguments) between the famously fiery couple. Frida and Diego lived with Frida's parents in the Blue House for most of their married lives from 1929-54. They created beautiful work in this warm, bright and simple environment. Entering Frida's Day bedroom, I look with intrigue into the actual mirror she painted herself in, that is positioned above a small single bed. Spending much of her adult life on her back, Frida had little choice but to look deep inside herself. In the loving surroundings of her family home she found the courage and strength to embrace her reality, and capture her innermost feelings of anguish, love and pain. Completely dependent on her family, painting may have been a way of regaining some control over her identity. She appeared to harness it as a weapon to reach people beyond her bed sheets where she was frequently held captive. Frida did not know she was a Surrealist until she was told by Andre Breton, a French writer and poet and founder of the Surrealism movement. Frida's voice whispers from the walls in quotes. "I paint because I need to, and I paint whatever passes through my head without any other consideration". "I don't paint dreams or nightmares, I paint my own reality."

I catch up with Chris in the final room of the house, Frida's Night bedroom. He narrowly avoids striking his camera against a large urn in the shape of a frog, which contains Frida's ashes. Her pet name for Diego was Frog. I smile at the thought of her resting inside Diego's belly. As we exit the doorway of La Casa Azul and return to the atmospheric streets of Coyoacan, I carry with me a feeling of alluring positivity. For a life so dark, here was a woman who shed a lot of light.

Opium with the Konyak King

The beat-up express bus overtakes a 4x4 on a blind bend. Cutting in sharply, we narrowly avoid a head-on collision with a truck heavily loaded with timber.

'He's totally lost it. I'm getting off!'

Chris holds on tightly to the seat in front. 'Different road rules here, remember.'

Speeding past the Behubar Tea Estate, a group of women wearing brightly coloured saris stand waist deep in a patchwork of green. This is not the first tea plantation we have seen in India, having spent the best part of a week now rolling around the less visited Northeast state of Assam. Jungle covered hills appear in the distance as we traverse the winding Dikhow River 30km from Sibsagar to the Assam-Nagaland border. I smile at the thought that the road to the end of the line was never supposed to be comfortable. The idea of travelling to Nagaland had been a complete accident. In fact, we hardly even knew it existed until we arrived in Kolkata. Discovering permit free entry was now possible to a region of India where tribal kings still rule, our plan was set. We desperately needed an adventure - a story to share. This had to be it.

At the foot of the Naga Hills we are approached by border police in the small frontier town of Naginimora. They escort us to a brick building and interrogate our passports. With minor confusion over the newly established permit policy, they eventually agree to allow us to continue on our journey to Mon, the largest settlement of any size in the less developed north of the region. Returning to the bus we are reminded of the troubles that once existed here in Nagaland, in the form of a rusty sign that states there is a ceasefire in the region. The driver of the bus appears stressed. The tourist hold-up has caused unscheduled delay. Powering the Ashok Leyland with his own personal anger, we leave Assam and enter a state of India that until fairly recently was off-limits to the curious tourist. Striking a pothole we are sent flying into the air. Completely airborne, shrieks of surprise are rapidly replaced by gasps and groans as our bodies return to rock hard seats.

I flash Chris a lion size grin. 'Broke the rules, Frank. Never sit at the back of the bus.'

We hit a second pothole. Chris is fired into the air with more force this time, planting his head directly inside one of the speaker holes. He leaves his mark in the form of a ceiling dent, and we exchange amused glances. A passenger who joined at the border begins to take interest in the comedy foreigners. I am immediately struck by his appearance. With small features and a wispy goatee beard he looks more similar to the people of Southeast Asia. He asks where we are from, and reveals he is travelling from Guwahati, the capital of Assam, to the village where he was born close to Mon. Following endless switchback corners on the unpaved track through the rainforest, we pass a factory with a chimney spewing thick black smoke into the atmosphere.

'Plywood,' he smiles. 'My uncle, he is working there.'

A short distance from Mon, he points out a rock face approximately thirty feet high that rises above the jungle from the road.

'In the past, the Konyak chief, he would throw criminals to their death here.'

'Seriously?' I reply.

'The Naga people, we are tribal. The killing of outcasts was once normal.'

Chris appears fascinated. 'We had the death penalty in England until not all that long ago. Difficult to imagine the Queen doing it herself though!'

'My friend's father lives in your country. He moved there in nineteen sixty-two. We had many problems in Nagaland after the British left. People here wanted their own country, so we fought against the government.'

'We saw an old sign for the ceasefire at the border'

'Yes. We signed a peace agreement in the Seventies. Unfortunately, tribal violence continues.'

'Is it dangerous?'

'No. Not for you. We are friendly. But of course you should take care. Normally tourists travelling this region, they are with a guide.'

A violent jolt signals that we have arrived at our destination. We scramble off the bus and plant our feet firmly on Naga soil. Chris negotiates a ride in a jeep taxi to the only accommodation in town. An expanding rural-urban centre with a population of around 16,000, the palm leaf and bamboo walled huts we had seen in villages on route are replaced by concrete and brick houses. Mon is the capital of the region and a central location for the coronation of Anghs, the chiefs of a network of tribes that control the north. Looping around the settlement, Chris points out a Baptist Church on top of a hill. Although the people of Nagaland were animist by tradition, over the past century almost 98% of the population have embraced Christianity following the influence of English missionaries.

We are met at the door of Helsa Cottage by an attentive Konyak woman with a friendly smile. She introduces herself as Aunty. Offering us a room at a mid-range price, we eat a substantial meal of rice, vegetables, pork and fish. The power cuts out minutes after the sun goes down. Aunty lights candles and explains that power and water in Mon is an unpredictable supply.

'The infrastructure put in place by the British in India didn't quite reach Nagaland,' she sighs.

Chris asks if Mon has changed much while she has been living here. Aunty looks surprised by his question. She explains it is completely unrecognisable. When she first arrived in Mon as a child in the 1960s there were no roads at all. She was carried from the plains on the back of a porter and greeted by people who wore no clothes.

With no time to waste, we arrange a jeep and a guide to take us to a tribal village on the border with Myanmar. I collect a bucket of hot water from the kitchen and make my way to bed. Looking out over Mon from the balcony, I see flickering candles on neighbouring rooftops. It is blissfully quiet and the sound of children singing can be heard faintly in the distance.

* * *

Up with the birds, I leave Si to arrange the logistics of our journey and sprint down to the local shop. I am served by an older gentleman who is wearing a threadbare suit jacket. He has a mouth full of red stained teeth like a vampire. Rolling areca nut inside betel leaf, he introduces me to pann, which is commonly chewed as a stimulant in India. A young guy sporting a Teddy boy quiff educates me about cherry and coconut pann, fire pann (which is literally ablaze when it enters your mouth), and even sex pann (popular with nervous men on their wedding night).

Si approaches with a crease running down the side of his face.

'Visit from the hair fairy during the night?' I laugh.

'Did Alon ask you about a gift for the king?'

'A gift? Like gold, frankincense and myrrh?'

'Chris, he's not the baby Jesus. I gave him five-hundred rupees. We can sort it out later.'

Exiting town we climb into the forested hills.

Alon shoots a smile over his shoulder. 'It is forty-two kilometres to the border with Myanmar.'

'Very close!' Si replies.

'Nagaland is one of the smallest states in India, so nowhere is very far away. Travel can be challenging, though. This road is quite new, so it is one of the easier routes for me to show you some of the traditional life here. Have you been to Burma?'

'No, not yet. A few years ago we travelled along the eastern border in southern China and northern Laos. We were photographing the tribal markets there. What's the population of Nagaland?'

'Approximately two million. Sixteen tribes, each with their own distinct culture, language and dress.'

We pass a cluster of bamboo houses surrounded by lush green paddy fields. Violet flowers carpet the forest floor between areca trees. A party of Konyak women wearing orange and red beads wander along the roadside with long sticks and baskets on their heads.

'Life for many people in this region is very different to the rest of India,' Alon continues. 'The Naga people are still living like the old times. In the village we are about to visit the local men they routinely smoke opium. It is a tradition that has become an important part of Konyak culture since it was introduced by the British during colonial times.'

'The British?' Si replies.

'Of course. For many centuries Indian farmers were forced by the British East India Company to grow poppy.'

'We didn't invent it though, did we? The people of Egypt and the Middle East were smoking opium many thousands of years ago.'

After a strong debate about opium, we learn that in the 1700s opium use in China was growing steadily in popularity. Britain's thirst for tea meant that during this period our country of origin was importing from China far more than it was exporting. The result was a critical depletion of Britain's silver stocks. To correct the balance, the East India Company, who had the monopoly on trade in China, began to mass produce opium in the nearby Indian state of Bengal and ship it to China. The Chinese made the trade illegal, but the company instead began to sell opium to smaller traders who then smuggled it into the country. Causing further disruption to China's tea market, Britain eventually began to establish its own tea estates in Assam and rapidly became one of the world's largest suppliers of black tea that was favoured in Europe.

Climbing steadily in altitude, houses and settlements slowly disappear. We pull over at the roadside to stretch our legs and scan an eerie barren landscape. Si points out how the forests have been heavily logged for miles around, with the odd charred tree stump existing as a reminder that there was once a forest covering this entire region. Making our way closer to the Myanmar border, we see a tribal Konyak man with a tattooed face. He is stripped to the waist and has a muzzle-loading gun over his shoulder.

'The Konyak manufacture these guns themselves,' Alon reveals, 'and gunpowder, too. They use them to hunt wild cat and small mammals for food and fur.'

Si appears completely awe-struck. 'They have tattoos on their faces like the Māori people of New Zealand.'

'Yes, they use a natural ink found here in the jungle. It is made using the resin of a toona ciliata tree. You may know it as red cedar. Different tattoos convey a person's status, position, stage of life and achievements in Konyak society.'

We pass a teenage boy wearing jeans and a pullover. He looks up as we pass.

'See the machete in his hand?' Alon smiles. 'It's called a dao. The Konyak men were using these knives for headhunting as recently as the late nineteen-sixties.'

Si lowers his camera. 'Headhunting? Hunting the head of what?'

'Konyak enemies. You did not know this?'

I catch myself massaging my throat. 'Our guidebook ran out after Assam.'

'The Celts practised headhunting along the Anglo-Scottish border until the late Middle Ages,' Si grins. 'Amazing how brutal life was here until not long before we were born.'

'What did they do with the heads?' I ask Alon.

'It was customary to preserve them as trophies.'

Passing a brand new road sign that points to Mon in one direction and Myanmar in the other, we find ourselves entering the village of Lungwa.

'The building on the hill with the flag on the top is a

military outpost. It marks the border between India and Myanmar.'

'Are we still in India?'

'Yes, partly. The tribal chief (the Angh) administers the entire village, but many young people serve in the Myanmarese army. Burma also runs schools in the section of the village that lies under its jurisdiction.'

Approaching a long bamboo structure with thatched palm leaf roofing, my mouth begins to feel unusually dry. I attempt to clear my throat causing Si deep irritation.

He thrusts a bottle of water in my face. 'Please, drink this.'

Two men appear in the doorway to the longhouse. Alon steps forward and introduces us to the Angh and the village council chairman. We all shake hands. The tribal chief is wearing a cowboy hat decorated with wild cat fur, and a khaki shirt. A necklace hangs around his neck depicting five heads cast in bronze. Invited inside, we enter a large dimly lit room with a hard earth floor and join three additional Konyak men sat around a central fireplace. The entire face of one of the men is covered in tattoos. A painfully thin old woman with a shaved head works in the shadows. She is sat near to shelving that contains a collection of rusty old tin cans and a mix and match of crockery. One guy pokes the fire, while the tattooed guy cleans an opium pipe. The third younger guy sits silently listening, he darts occasional glances at me and Si. The chief converses with Alon. I am fascinated to hear the Konyak language, which is a Sino-Tibetan language that is predominantly spoken in the east of Nagaland.

Alon looks over at us with his head slightly bowed. 'Please, I would like to present to you the Angh's son and heir.'

Si shakes hands with the proud looking boy sat beside him.

Next Alon fishes a bottle of whiskey out of his bag. 'This is the Angh's favourite whiskey,' Alon explains, 'a gift from you.'

The king gladly accepts the bottle and, without hesitation, he cracks the lid and pours the contents into two mugs with a red love heart design. The Angh sips the strong alcohol and avoids all eye contact. I feel immediate pangs of guilt. This is the kind of tourism we detested, where the interaction of the foreigner has a direct impact on the local people. Getting the local tribal king drunk was never part of our plan. I imagine more tourists following in our footsteps, an ever-increasing flow of adventure seekers bringing gifts of whisky and influencing the future outcome of a man, who has a great responsibility to the people living in this region. With barely enough time to digest breakfast, the opium comes out. Si leans forward and watches with keen interest, as the men tend to the fire and prepare the long wooden pipe. Above the fireplace, a metal rack is attached to the ceiling for smoking meat and hanging cooking pots over the flames. Presumably for decoration, wild cat tails are slung over the sides and a collection of small mammal skulls fill a metal tray. The ceiling of the longhouse is covered in thick black tar that has accumulated over many years. The guy with the tattoo prepares a dry organic fibre used for smoking and smears brown opium paste onto a metal spoon before holding it over the fire. It rapidly turns to liquid and begins to bubble. With the assistance of the council chairman, the fibre is then soaked in the liquid opium. Poking it into the neck of the carved wooden pipe, he holds a piece of red hot charcoal to the end and the chairman inhales a deep lungful of smoke. The pipe is refilled and passed around the room. The chief begins to relax and a broad smile inches across his face.

* * *

A tap on the shoulder draws my gaze away from the hypnotic fire. Chris looms above me. On a cloud of opium smoke, we make a journey around the longhouse with Alon and the king's son.

Alon peers up at the ceiling. 'This central totem pillar extends above the thatched roof. It divides the house into two countries. The Angh takes his meals in India and sleeps in Myanmar.'

Stepping across the invisible boundary into Myanmar, the future tribal chief proudly leads us over to a display of large brass gongs. They are hung on the wall next to a collection of deer antlers and buffalo skulls with enormous devil horns. Chris looks in awe at a magnificent table-sized monument, with intricate carvings depicting a ferocious tiger and a hunter with a spear.

Alon speaks slowly with a hushed voice. 'There is a similar monument to this one in the nearby village of Shangnyu. It is believed by the Konyak to be constructed by heavenly angels. The legend tells of an outcast who the Angh threw down a cliff to kill him after he had committed a crime against the community, but the fall had failed to kill him. According to the story, the outcast had started cutting down trees and carving objects on them. The villagers could hear the sounds of many people working together, but when they approached the site where he was working they found him alone. It is believed that he was helped in his work by these heavenly angels.'

Golden sunlight streams through the entrance of the longhouse, and we examine a display of tribal jewellery neatly spaced out on woven matting. I squat down and take a closer look.

'The Konyak are adept artisans and skilled craftsmen,' Alon reveals. 'They carve designs on the wooden handles of their weapons, and create beaded headgear and necklaces.'

A couple of local women watch curiously from the doorway.

'The Naga women, they are very beautiful,' Alon grins. 'The former tribal chief of the village had sixty wives. His jurisdiction extended north from here all the way along the Myanmar border to the Indian state of Arunachal Pradesh.'

Chris purchases a tribal necklace with a bronze pendant in the form of a head.

'Is that how many people you've killed?' I wink.

He looks shocked. 'Is that what it means?'

Alon fights a smile. 'Trophies were once real human heads. I guess they may still symbolise to some of the Konyak people how many enemies they have killed.'

'I won't actually wear it, then,' Chris smiles. 'I'll keep it as a souvenir.'

'Good plan,' I laugh.

Exiting the longhouse, we look down from the ridge over the thick Burmese jungle. I try to imagine all of the colourful species of birds and butterflies, monkeys and snakes that inhabit this sub-tropical region of the world. We take a stroll around the tranquil settlement of Lungwa and meet a local family living in the village. One of the kids carries her infant baby sister in a sling on her back.

'The elder children are given the responsibility of taking care of their brothers and sisters,' smiles Alon. 'They help with the daily chores of drying corn and collecting firewood. It is a tough life growing up here.

Much work to do.'

Returning to the jeep parked up outside the longhouse, we are surprised to be met by a rather serious looking guy wearing a white shirt, black trousers and shiny leather shoes. His smart appearance looks quite alien in our tribal jungle setting. He turns out to be a Burmese immigration official and jots down our names and passport numbers in a book before hurrying away. The Konyak king, his son and the tribal chairman stand and watch from the entrance of the longhouse. We shake hands and thank them for permitting our visit. Carried away in the moment, Chris invites them all to visit our hometown of Daventry whenever they like. I smile at the thought of sitting in an English pub garden with the king drinking a traditional pint of real ale. The three men appear amused when Chris beats me to the front passenger seat of the 4x4. I gracefully accept defeat, and cast a salute before sliding into the back. The Angh's son bows his head, and I feel a strong sense of privilege for having had the chance to glimpse at a world that appeared to be on the precipice of dramatic change.

Approximately halfway down the mountain, we draw to an abrupt halt. Two large trucks heavily loaded with enormous felled trees attempt to squeeze past one another. Local women carrying baskets collect scraps of wood that have fallen to the ground. I watch with curiosity as a tribal man in his early seventies wanders out of the forest and joins a group of villagers close to where we are standing. He is carrying a tall spear and wearing an elaborate headdress of exotic Hornbill feathers. On tenterhooks, I'm half expecting this wise tribal elder to march into the middle of the road and strike his spear hard on the tarmac. "Enough!" he would cry. "Enough destruction of our land. From today no more trees will fall." Of course, he doesn't say that. He doesn't say anything at all.

Returning to Mon shortly before sunset, we stop for tea at Aunty's new place. Led around a well-kept garden, she explains how tourism has been on the increase in Nagaland for the past few years.

She turns to Chris, and raises her eyebrows. 'The accommodation here is aimed at catering to a more upmarket customer base. All of the rooms are en-suite.'

Tasting the Naga red chilli, allegedly the hottest in the world, and drinking more fire quenching Naga black tea, we are left to relax in the garden and listen to the soothing sounds of the birdlife in the trees. We take a moment to contemplate Nagaland and the wonderfully colourful Konyak people, who we have had the pleasure of meeting during our brief visit here. It seems fairly clear life in Nagaland is on the up. The boom time in India is reaching the far corners of its frontiers and creating a lucrative industry for some, with the sale of its natural resources. But what price will the Naga people pay for the environmental destruction of their tribal homeland, and how will this affect the lives of the ordinary rural communities in this region living simple and self-sufficient lives? In order to protect their best interests the people of Nagaland, who have earned a reputation for being fiercely independent, will need to debate the future of their fragile territory carefully and move intelligently, unselfishly and with caution towards the promise of a more economically prosperous future.

Up the Etna

The bow door slowly opens like the yawn of a metal monster, revealing the clear night sky and the bright lights of Messina harbour. Buzzing with anticipation, I imagine I'm Richard the Lionheart, well, he did arrive in Sicily by ship in 1190, and cast a sturdy salute at the unshaven guy wearing a hi-viz who frantically waves us off the ferry. The clank of the iron ramp on the quayside signals the start of our road trip around the Mediterranean's largest island. On a map, Sicily resembles a ball being kicked towards North Africa by Totti's boot – it's a winning goal for an island that over the centuries has absorbed Greek, Spanish, French and Arab influences into its culture and cuisine. Quicker than the word "arancini" (rice balls stuffed with bacon) rolls off the tongue, we join the fast flowing traffic leading to the heart of the city along Palazzo del Monte di Pietà. Considering Messina was flattened by an earthquake in 1908 and carpet bombed by the Allies in 1943, it's a relief to see the Duomo di Messina is still standing.

I tap a page in the guidebook. 'Did you know the cathedral in this city has the world's largest astronomical clock?'

Si cuts sharply in front of a speeding truck. 'An astronomically large what?'

'Clock.'

Concern radiates from my brother's troubled face. 'You do realise Mount Etna erupted only a few weeks ago. The Sicilian authorities completely shut down Catania airport.'

'It was a puff of smoke.'

'A puff of smoke? Chris, it was so colossal it could be seen from space. Etna was known to the Greeks as the realm of Vulcan God of Fire. It's the second most active volcano in the world.'

I flash a smile. 'As long as it doesn't melt our gelatos!'

Mission

Drive full circle around an island at the toe of Italy's boot, feast on Sicilian culinary delights, explore mind-blowing history, and conclude our journey hanging out with the dead in Palermo's eerie catacombs.

Destination

Sicily. An island famed for its alluring beauty, ancient ruins, legends of sea monsters and the one-eyed cyclops, origins of the sonnet, Greek mathematician Archimedes, the Sicilian mafia, and last but not least the Teatro Massimo (largest opera house in Italy).

Route

Sail from mainland Italy by ship to the ancient port city of Messina, cruise the east coast to glamorous Taormina, power to the top of the highly active Mount Etna volcano, explore myths in Syracuse, mosaics at the Roman Villa del

Casale, soak our weary bones off the Turkish Steps and end our journey with friends in the gritty city streets of Palermo.

Risk factor

Blown up by a volcano, crushed by a 3,000-year-old Greek column, eat too much delicious food and die.

Vehicle

Rover 214. Winning bid on eBay for $400. Assembled at the Longbridge plant in Birmingham the year the Iraqi forces invaded Kuwait and Margaret Thatcher, the Iron Lady, resigned as UK Prime Minister. The movie *Dances with Wolves* with Kevin Costner was a big hit and 'Something Happened On The Way To Heaven' by Phil Collins was blaring out of every Pioneer LP turntable around the world. Yep, the car was born in the year 1990. Ok, so maybe it's not exactly the coolest vehicle, but Si found a Bee Gees greatest hits album stuck in the tape player, and it has a luxurious cream interior, faux wood dash, a handy coins tray and all four wheels roll. What more could two knuckleheads ask for?

* * *

Perched on a rocky promontory high over the ancient bay of Giardini Naxos, we trot across the chequered tiles of Piazza IX Aprile to a pavement cafe.

'Great location to launch our adventure,' Chris beams, slipping on his shades.

'You can say that again, matey. Taormina was once a haven for stars of the silver screen. Elizabeth Taylor, Cary

Grant, Audrey Hepburn and Marlon Brando, they all used to hang out here in the nineteen-fifties.'

'Difficult to imagine being in such company.'

'Would you want to be?'

'Absolutely, yes.'

'Are you sure? Pretentious dinner parties, shallow stars brimming with self-importance.'

'The wine,' Chris winks, adjusting the collar of his uncharacteristically smart shirt.

'What time's the board meeting?'

'Mock all you like, pal. I'm upping the game.'

'We're on a road trip. You live in a car.'

'Don't be such a pessimist.'

Eager to explore an island at the furthest point south of Italy's boot, we leap aboard our 90s executive saloon. With lively tarantella flute music blasting from the speakers, we zigzag through orchards of lemons and figs in the upper part of the Valle del Bove. Making a pit stop in the small rural community of Zafferana Etnea, Chris stocks up on locally produced almonds, walnuts and giant peaches bursting with Sicilian sunshine. Entering the Mount Etna National Park, the engine of the Rover purrs like an old lioness, as the forested landscape morphs into eerie volcanic rock. With dramatic views into the valley below, we battle through the larval blackness at an elevation of around 2,000 metres. On the approach to Refugio Sapienza, I'm curious to know what is about to slide into view. A snapshot from 230 million years ago during the Triassic period? We reach the brow of a hill, but sadly our illusions of being surrounded by spewing lava and theropods are dashed when we arrive at a really busy car park crammed full of campervans and tour coaches.

* * *

Outside the entrance to the visitors centre, Si falls into conversation with a Canadian couple from Manitoba. Donovan is a brave firefighter with colourful tattoos and a cowboy moustache, and Brigitte is a professional yoga teacher with electric blue eyes. They are on a two week tour of Europe.

'If the mountain blows its top, I'm staying right here,' Donovan nods vehemently. 'Finish my coffee at these prices.'

Brigitte shakes her head with irritation. She knows all too well the stubborn gorilla would do exactly that.

'Where did you guys meet?' Si asks, intrigued by this funky couple.

'In a snake queue.' Donovan turns to Brigitte and pulls a cheeky face.

'At a serpentarium?'

They both look at Si with a puzzled expression.

'It's a zoological exhibition for reptiles and amphibians.'

'You mean a herpetarium,' I add, with a smug grin.

Donovan releases a raucous laugh. 'Guys, what are you talking about? We met at Las Vegas airport six years ago. We were checking in for our flight to Winnipeg. No snakes on the plane.'

Brigitte tilts her head to one side and flashes a 'they're-so-stupid-but-so-cute' smile.

'We made eye contact at every turn in the line,' Donovan continues. 'By the time we reached the check-in desk we were practically engaged. I was trying to play it cool and blew my chance of talking to her, but as if by magic her seat was right next to mine on the flight.'

'A miracle!' Brigitte sings. They both gaze dreamily into each other's eyes.

Due to the recent eruption the cable car to the very top of Mount Etna is closed. Si suggests we make a circuit around accessible areas of the lower viewpoints. We end our tour back at the visitors centre. I read about American military efforts in 1992 to prevent a flow of lava from destroying Zafferana Etnea. During Operation Volcano Buster, seven-ton concrete blocks were dropped from powerful C-53 helicopters in an attempt to plug the vent with 92 tons of concrete and rubble. Sadly, after a few days the lava started to move again destroying vineyards and setting fire to fruit trees.

I turn to Donovan. 'Good job you're a firefighter.'

'Lava is out of my league, man.' He circles a finger in the air. 'Chopper out of here.'

'After your coffee?'

'Coffee first every time.'

'My only experience of fire is knocking back shots of flaming Sambuca and campfires on road trips with Si.'

The buffalo-sized Canadian drops his smile. 'I could never travel with my brother. You guys fight?'

'Sure, sometimes, but when you're on a journey you kind of have to get along.'

'I once shared a mining camp in the Yukon with a hundred men. You soon realise everyone is unbearable. Life gets easier once you accept that.'

We join Si and Brigitte by the Rover.

'Need a ride?' I smile.

Donovan roars with laughter. 'No thanks, guys. Our luxury minibus takes us directly back to the hotel. Anyways, not sure we'd make it in this.'

'What are you talking about? This motor was top of the range back in the day,' Si proudly reveals, 'heated seats, electric sunroof, enormous glove compartment.'

Brigitte sprawls across the hood. 'I'm not planning on

wearing gloves, but I love it!' she giggles, reaching her arms above her head.

'It's certainly vintage, man.'

Brigitte looks dreamily up at the sky. 'Where will you go now?'

'Heading south,' I reply, pointing across the barren landscape towards Syracuse. 'Our finish line is the Catacombs in Palermo.'

Donovan looks amused. 'Hanging out with the dead?'

'Yes, but we are also meeting the living. An old friend from Milan.'

Brigitte tilts her head to the side in that characteristically sympathetic way of hers, and smiles. 'Ah, that's so cute. I think it's an awesome idea.' She wraps herself around Donovan's barrel chest. 'Just because we're ending our vacation on the Côte d'Azur drinking cocktails doesn't mean everyone has to.'

With open invites to visit Manitoba we take a few selfies, exchange Instagram accounts and group hug before making our way back down the volcano. Si travels in a painfully low gear in a bid to slow our descent. Forced to hammer the brakes through endless hairpin bends and switchback corners, I look in surprise when I see thick black smoke pouring from beneath the car.

'Pull over!' I yell.

Fearing the Rover may catch fire and explode in a huge fireball, we sprint for the cover of a nearby rock. Poking our heads into view we take a peek at the ticking time bomb.

'What about my stuff?'

Si frowns. 'The junk in the trunk?'

I consider defending my possessions, but then realise I agree, it is all pretty much junk. After an hour of chilling in the sunshine, we feel confident to inspect the damage.

Si gingerly pours water over the brake disks that are glowing red. Quenched by the cool mountain water they hiss and steam rises. The sun flickers low behind the trees as the day swaps shifts with the night. It is getting late, so we decide to put up the tent and spend the night on the mountain.

* * *

We celebrate the car not exploding with a dunk in the sea, closely followed by a delicious chub mackerel breakfast. Beating Chris to the wheel, I wrestle free of the traffic around Catania's enormous fish market and drive south to Syracuse. Tucked away in the southeast corner of Sicily, Syracuse is a 2,700 year old architectural treasure trove that was once a major power of the Mediterranean world. We cross a bridge over a narrow channel to the island of Ortigia.

Chris flashes a smile. 'Guess who was born here?'

'Al Pacino?'

'Nope.'

'Pavarotti?'

'No.'

'Marco Polo?'

'Wrong again.'

'I give up.'

'Archimedes!'

'Incredible. Is this where he ran naked through the streets shouting "*eureka*!"?'

'That's right, Si. The ancestors of people living here saw his bare bottom. The poor bloke was run through with a sword by a Roman soldier at the age of seventy-five.'

Exploring on foot, we buy fresh fruit from the buzzing Ortigia market where the aromas of spices, almonds and chilli peppers tingle our nostrils. Chris invests in a portion of u strattu, delicious crushed tomatoes and a loaf of freshly baked Sicilian sesame seed bread. We navigate a maze of narrow alleyways to the Temple of Apollo. All that remains of one of the most important ancient Greek monuments on Ortigia are rectangular foundations, stone walls and a dozen or more crumbling columns. Chris hides his smile at hearing an overweight tourist refer to the ancient temple as "a pile of old rocks". Snacking on pomegranates, we soak up the Doric atmosphere under a scorching hot sun. I try to imagine how the city may have looked before it was destroyed by a massive earthquake and rebuilt in typical Sicilian Baroque style. Syracuse was once revered for its beauty and prestige on a par with Athens. In fact, in its heyday it was the largest city in the ancient world, bigger than Athens and Corinth combined. Wandering around Piazza del Duomo, we peek inside the colossal cathedral, built on the site where the ancient Temple of Athena once stood. We end our time in Syracuse on the waterfront, and walk the full length of the ancient harbour along Passeggio Adorno to the Fountain of Arethusa. Eating gelato, we discover that in Greek mythology the natural spring here is where the nymph Arethusa returned to Earth's surface after escaping from her undersea home in Arcadia. The Greeks certainly had some colourful ideas. Keen not to slop ice cream down the front of his smart tailored shorts, Chris sits on the harbour wall with his feet wide apart. He proceeds to share the bizarre story of Asteria. According to the legend, her sister Leto was the bride of Zeus. Not only did she transform herself into a quail, she then threw herself into the sea and metamorphosed into this very island. Watching the sun sink low in the sky, flooding the surrounding buildings in soft tangerine light, we pull ourselves away from the lure

142

of Syracuse and return to the open road.

Travelling inland we rise into the Hyblean Mountains. At the heart of the Pergusa nature reserve, Chris identifies a lake on the map where we can set up base for the night and enjoy a quick swim. I stand ankle deep in the muddy shallows and splash reed choked water, the consistency of spinach soup, over my head and face. Hanging out with the waterfowl, we dine al fresco on a feast of Sicilian sardines and anchovies served with black olives and piacentinu cheese salad. Between sips of robust country wine, Chris proceeds to share stories about La Stidda (The Star), a splinter group of the long established Sicilian mafia.

'How do you identify a member of La Stidda?' he asks, his face illuminated in the flickering candlelight.

'Patent leather shoes? Slicked back hair?'

'Nope, a tattoo of a five-pointed star on the right hand between the thumb and index finger. There was a brutal mafia war in the early nineties. Over three-hundred people were killed. Gruesome acts of violence and torture plagued this region. Fingernails were torn out, digits removed, children of gangsters dissolved in acid.'

I hear a noise in the reeds behind me and dart a paranoid glance over my shoulder.

'It is small fry, though, in comparison to the brutality of the ancient past,' Chris continues. 'The thought of the brazen bull literally sends shivers down my spine.'

'Brazen bull?'

'It was an ancient Greek torture and execution device designed for Phalaris. He was the Sicilian tyrant of Akragas, a port city further along the coast. The bull was life-size and believed to have been made entirely from bronze. The condemned, if it was ever used, were forced to climb through a small hatch into a hollow chamber inside the bull. They would be kept there for days, even weeks. On the day of execution a large fire was lit beneath it. When the bronze bull heated up the prisoners trapped inside were slow-roasted alive. According to legend, the head of the bull contained acoustic apparatus.'

'So it was also a musical instrument?'

'Si, the brazen bull was in no way a "let's all sing songs around the campfire" musical instrument. No, my friend. The job of the acoustic apparatus was to convert the screams of those imprisoned inside.'

'Convert them into what?'

'The terrifying sound of an infuriated bellowing bull. The frightening noise would only increase in volume with the prisoner's desperate cries for mercy.'

I collapse into the car around midnight and check the doors are locked three or four times. Slightly traumatised by Chris's horror stories of brutal torture, I attempt to flood my mind with happy thoughts of the beautiful countryside we have driven through today. I see movement close to a cluster of trees. Chris is already snoring like a beast. This is going to be a long night.

* * *

Si explodes out of the pea green water. A surprised moorhen takes flight. I continue to shave in the wing mirror while the swamp monster wrestles to get dressed. Throwing the cooking equipment into the back of the car we drive a few kilometres south. We stop on route at a bakery to buy fresh cannoli pastries pumped full of thick cream. Making a circuit around the settlement of Piazza Armerina, with its enormous baroque cathedral at its centre, we push on to the nearby Unesco Villa Romana del Casale.

'What is this place, a museum?' Si asks.

'You don't sound very enthusiastic.'

He shrugs. 'Maybe I was expecting something a bit more adventurous after driving up an active volcano.'

'Fear not, buddy. This place is going to blow your mind. There are over forty rooms covered by intricate mosaic tiles. Archaeologists travel here from all over the world. It's the daddy of Roman mosaic art. You have to understand, this villa is very relevant to our journey. It has survived earthquakes, floods, fires and the collapse of an empire.'

'Are there toilets inside?'

'Are you listening to a word I'm saying?'

Si thrusts a hand in the air and marches urgently across the car park. In the entrance to the villa I get pounced on by a local guide. Alessandro is a smooth talking character with exceptionally white teeth. He reveals that the nearby town of Piazza Armerina was established during the Norman Conquest.

'Everywhere you travel in Sicily the people are different,' he beams. 'Here we speak a Gallo-Italic dialect similar to the Lombards from northern Italy. You know, you can find traces of Greek, Arabic, French, Catalan and Spanish all on one island. We are a rich mix, a fruity cocktail. We have everything you need here in Sicily. Would you like a guide?'

'No, thank you.'

Following an awkward moment of silence, a young family wanders into view. Alessandro makes his excuses and scurries over to them. Transported back in time to the world of the Roman Empire, we walk along elevated walkways through the ruins of a villa that was once the residence of emperor Maximianus. Si appears transfixed, as we try to imagine the 12th century earthquake that shook this building apart. Incredibly, the colourful mosaics that adorn most of the rooms were preserved by a mudslide. They survived in almost pristine condition until they were rediscovered by archaeologists around 700 years later. Completely spellbound by the art that was created here during this fascinating period of the Roman Empire, we step into what was the Gymnasium and then enter an octagonal hall decorated with mosaics depicting Amorini fishermen hauling in their catch from small boats. Another scene depicts a marine procession with fish, a lobster, ducks, a squid, a snake and a couple of winged-angels. The massage room is next, with the portrait of an athlete being rubbed down with oil. Two muscular slaves stand strong in the foreground, their names Titus and Cassius written on loincloth tied around their waists. Reading the information boards, it is thought North African mosaic workers were responsible for the portrayal of scenes of fighting wild beasts, in addition to illustrations of other exotic animals such as elephants, lions, tigers and camels. Other depictions show armed figures carrying large shields and riding horse-drawn chariots, and a race for the children with smaller chariots pulled by pigeons, ducks, flamingos and various other waterfowl. One of the final works of art inside the large Roman villa reveals a group of women wearing two-piece bikini garments worn during competitive athletic events. We find great comfort in the thought that the bikini has been around for over 1,600 years.

Experiencing Roman mosaic overload, we emerge from the villa and drive 100km south to the coast and the Scala dei Turchi (Stair of the Turks). Si chews the fat with a surfer dude from Portugal, who is relaxing in the shade of his VW campervan. I skip down to the ocean and dive into the crystal clear water, a shoal of stripy fish dart between the rocks. A dark shape passes beneath me. I spin around and scan my surroundings for a fin. According to recent news reports, a great white shark had been spotted off the coast of Sicily. It would be just my luck to get bitten in half, and miss what is left of the olives and piacentinu cheese. I spot the mysterious shadow a second time. Panic rises through me as I tread water. "Swim like crazy back to shore, you blithering idiot!" A woman suddenly bursts out of the water. Her big brown eyes are magnified by a snorkel mask. She spits out the mouthpiece and beams a smile. It is love at first sight. I know instantly she is not a mermaid, because (a) mythological creatures like mermaids do not exist and (b) mermaids do not require a snorkel mask.

I break the silence. 'Hi, I'm Chris from England. Where are you from?'

She blinks and continues to smile, clearly not understanding a single word I am saying. After what feels like an hour of treading water, we both eventually swim over to dry land and drift our separate ways. I join the crowds of holidaymakers sucking up the vitamin D, and slip on my shades to shield my eyes from the blinding white rock. I find myself listening to a loud British tourist sitting nearby, who annoyingly proceeds to conjure up a list of every single country he has visited. Newfoundland is not a country, buddy. The girl sat next to him wrestles a yawn, as the conversation takes a major diversion down Monotone Street. The guy seems aware he is losing her attention, so he shifts up a gear and begins to waffle on about his life back home. He misses his mates, his dog and his high-pressure job in the City. Any moment now and I'm expecting her to yell out, "For Christ sake, Jeremy, shut the fuck up!" but instead they collapse into a passionate embrace and start kissing. I smile at the thought that if love were a beast in Greek mythology, it would be a strange four-legged creature that we should make no attempt to understand.

* * *

Spinning the car over to the Valle dei Templi, we look in awe at the staggeringly well-preserved Greek Temple of Concordia. Devouring a portion of couscous and prawns in the shade of an 800-year-old olive tree, we bid the ancient city of Akragas farewell, hop aboard our trusty chariot and cruise north on a deserted highway. Much to Chris' annoyance, the Bee Gees album wedged in the tape player kicks into life. I feel compelled to sing along.

'Whether you're a brother or whether you're a mother
You're stayin' alive, stayin' alive
Feel the city breakin' and everybody shakin'
And we're stayin' alive, stayin' alive
Ah, ha, ha, ha, stayin' alive, stayin' alive
Ah, ha, ha...'

Extending his index finger, Chris cuts the music dead…

Winding our way through the rugged interior of northwest Sicily, on the last leg of our journey to Palermo, the sky blackens. In normal circumstances a little precipitation isn't a problem, so long as your windscreen wipers work. The clouds burst open in a torrential downpour; we continue to drive until it becomes impossible to see. Somewhere in Sicily's agricultural heartland, Chris pulls over in the entrance to a large wheat field. I recline my seat and close my eyes. I take a moment to enjoy the sound of a million tiny fingers drumming on the roof of the car. My phone begins to buzz. I fumble in my pocket and answer the call.

'Hello?'

'Simon, it's Keanu from Hands4Job. How's it going, mate? Can you start tomorrow night? You'd be doing me a huge favour.'

'Tonight?'

'Yes, that'd be great, mate. Easy work. You got a forklift licence? Actually, it doesn't matter. You'll probably be emptying the bins, anyway. It's the new warehouse in Milton Keynes near the railway bridge just off the M1. Worked there before, mate?'

'No. Look, Keanu, I'm not...'

'It's a thirteen week contract. All goes well you'll be moved from bins to picking. Could be a job for life if you play your cards right. Bit of advice, though, don't stand around chatting. Grab a broom and do some sweeping. The supervisors are all ex-army. Know what I mean, mate? Top man.'

The line cuts dead.

Chris rolls his eyes. 'You're going to have to call him back.'

'I'm low on credits.'

'Don't piss off Keanu. We'll be back in England soon.'

'But I thought we were travel writers now?'

'Dial the frigging number.'

I release a deep sigh. Chris bursts open a sack of Taralli breadsticks. Emptying bins on a remote industrial estate in the dead of night could not be further from our minds right now. I shake my head despairingly, before forcing a large fistful of the snacks into my mouth.

The Sicilian adrenalin fuelled morning rush hour traffic kick-starts our day into action. Unsure if we are heading in the right direction, Chris swerves across two lanes of traffic triggering a chorus of car horns. I catch a glimpse in the wing mirror of the angry face of the driver behind. He presses the palms of his hands together in prayer and mimes "mamma mia". Arabian domes and bursts of baroque splendour shyly reveal themselves behind centuries-old apartment buildings. Keen to absorb every last ounce of inspiration from our Sicilian adventure, we freshen up in the hotel room and embark on a quest to get to the heart of one of the most edgy cities in Europe.

Marching through the sticky streets of Palermo, we make a spiral around the historic centre and seek out examples of Arab-Norman architecture that flourished here during Norman rule. The Church of San Cataldo, with its three red Arabic domes atop cubic towers, brings a smile to my face and we look in awe at the striking Palazzo dei Normanni, where beautiful Arabic arches and wooden honey-combed ceilings exist in harmony with Byzantine mosaics. Chris experiences near architectural orgasm as he leaps around Piazza Bellini. A late breakfast affords us the opportunity to taste almond and coffee flavoured granite, a creamy sorbet-style dessert scooped into freshly baked brioche. It is beyond delicious. Awakening our appetites, Chris warns that an Italian guy he once worked with in London returned from a trip to Sicily with a face so fat his head literally tilted to one side. The old quarter of Ballaro lures us with the promise of experiencing the grittier side of the city. We weave through a maze of narrow backstreets brimming with street art, and duck beneath sweet-smelling laundry strung between apartment buildings. Many Bangladeshi and West Africans migrated to Italy in the 1980s, and settled here in the Ballaro district. A second wave of migration had begun in recent times since civil crisis erupted in nearby Libya. Over a thousand mile stretch of unpoliced Libyan coastline was now ripe for migrant smugglers since the death of Colonel Gaddafi.

We arrive at the famous Ballaro food market, one of four markets in Palermo that has been in existence since the 11th century. We browse stalls selling everything imaginable, fresh vegetables, blood oranges, spices, seafood, pine nuts, raisins, almonds, local sun ripened tomatoes, lemons and the finest olive oil. Market traders shout the loudest to compete at grabbing attention and drawing in the customers. Unable to resist the mouth-watering aromas, we gorge on sfincione (thick slices of squishy bread heaped with fresh tomato sauce, onions and cheese) and battle over a portion of panelli, crispy squares of deep-fried chickpeas. The rustic Sicilian flavours have our taste buds performing summersaults. Chris invests in a portion of stuffed potato crocchè, together with a healthy serving of caponata (an aubergine dish) to sample later.

* * *

We nurse our swollen stomachs in a bustling pavement cafe. Two smartly dressed women participate in an animated debate at the counter.

Si leans forward. 'Apparently, the government are slowly taking back laundered mob money and injecting it into the city. Money from pizzo.'

A palermitano sat at the next table peers over his newspaper. The large antique espresso machine hisses and whistles before gurgling noisily, as the barista pumps steam into a pitcher of milk.

'Listen to this,' I whisper, darting glances around the café. 'In Palermo the other day, an Italian mafia boss was shot in the head whilst riding his bicycle through the city.'

'Please tell me he wasn't wearing trouser clips.'

'No idea, but the police said it was a warning that Cosa

Nostra is far from beaten.' I point my teaspoon at Si. 'What does Cosa Nostra mean?'

'Our Thing.'

'Been doing your homework,' I smile, grabbing a handful of sugar sachets. The guy reading the newspaper stares directly at me. I wait for him to look away before slipping them into my pocket. 'Hey, Si, maybe we should start our own mafia racket thingy. You know, pimp up our lives.'

'We don't have the right skills. Besides, I'm a pacifist and you'd totally freak out if you got blood on your shirt.' Si leans back in his chair and attempts to impersonate Marlon Brando in *The Godfather*. "Revenge is a dish best served cold." Still in character he takes a sip of coffee, but quickly recoils. 'Oh, flipping heck that's hot.'

Pumped full of caffeine we make a speedy hike to the opulent Teatro Massimo, the biggest and most important opera house in the whole of Italy. Si whips out his camera and steals one or two sneaky shots of the grand reception hall, while I stand between the Greek columns and keep an eye out for Lucia.

'Crissy!' a voice calls out.

I turn to see Lucia running up the steps. A girl with purple hair and a sharply cut fringe trails behind.

'So crazy we're in Sicily at the same time!' I smile, giving Lucia a big hug.

'I know! When I saw your photographs I couldn't believe it.' Lucia puts an arm around her friend. 'This is my Greta. She is an artist. We are a couple.'

'A couple? Oh, wow, you look so great together,' I reply, hiding my surprise.

'How do you know Lucia?' Greta asks, chewing on gum.

'We met in Olinda a few years ago. It was carnival. We

were dancing and drinking cachaça. Brazil's street parties are amazing.'

Greta looks me up and down. 'Why are you wearing a shirt? You go to the office?'

'No, I'm on a road trip.'

'I love your new style,' Lucia giggles. 'You look very mature.'

'You mean old,' Si smirks.

'It's sad we only have a short time together. You must visit Milan. We have a beautiful apartment with a spare room.'

Greta shakes her head vehemently. 'The spare room is my art studio.'

'Hey, no problem. We can get a hotel.'

'You said about visiting the catacombs,' Lucia sings, quickly changing the subject.

'Yes, I need to see this place. It's supposed to be...'

'Depressing,' Si laughs.

Greta's eyes light up. It seems she too is curious to take a sneaky peek at Sicily's notorious display of the dead. We skip down the steps of the grand theatre to a nearby bus stop.

Lucia spins around on her heels. 'Please, guys, wait here. We use the bathroom in the restaurant across the street.'

The girls cling to one another as they seize a break in the traffic.

Si turns to me. 'Change your shirt. You look so uncomfortable.'

'There's not enough time!'

'You've got huge sweat marks under your pits. Do it!'

I search frantically through my possessions and seize a scruffy old t-shirt that's wrapped around my camera.

'Quick, you dumbass, they're coming back! Wait a

minute, what are all those little black dots on your face.'

Discovering the print on the t-shirt has melted in the heat, I frantically pour water over my head and start scrubbing. The girls rock up and laugh hysterically. I am soaking wet through and wearing a t-shirt two sizes too small with a tear exposing my right nipple.

* * *

We hurtle through the city streets aboard a packed bus. Chris looks a thousand times more comfortable wearing a casual t-shirt purchased from a nearby souvenir shop. The slogan, "I can't keep calm I'm Sicilian!" is emblazoned across the front. At the entrance of the infamous Catacombe dei Cappuccini, a grey-faced gentleman leads us to the subterranean world that lies beneath the streets of Palermo. We find ourselves in an underground cavern that is overflowing with literally hundreds of corpses. In the 19th century, over eight-thousand Palermo citizens were laid to rest in these catacombs. Natural light delivered through vents illuminates the segregated galleries as we look in awe at endless rows of embalmed corpses strung on the walls, or laid outstretched on shelves. Prelates (high-ranking members of the clergy) were the first to be preserved in the catacombs. They were later joined by notables and their families until the practise was ended in 1880. The bodies are eerily wearing clothes of the period when they died. Priests are dressed in clerical vestments, and important men of the city are wearing their finest suits and waistcoats. Wealthy women model hats, bonnets and contemporary fashion of the day. The rather grim job of preserving the bodies was carried out by the Capuchin monks, who would first haul out their entrails before leaving them to dehydrate for several months. The deceased would then be bathed in vinegar and herbs before being sun dried like a raisin.

Growing steadily accustomed to our new lives in the company of the dead, Chris and Lucia take interest in the shoes, hats, handkerchiefs and cravats. Imagine a vintage fashion and textile museum with actual dead bodies instead of mannequins. Many of the skeletal faces appear to chat in frozen conversation, while others look more frightening with long wispy hair and moustaches that appear to have continued to grow long after they passed away. Greta stands inches away from a woman of high society, who wears a white dress with layered skirts. In contrast to Greta's gothic punk image, which includes piercings, purple highlights and skinny jeans, their extreme difference in appearance creates the illusion of time travel. Chris waves me over to a dimly lit cavern. We peer at a macabre scene of skeletal monks wearing brown hooded robes that are surrounded by hundreds of artistically arranged human skulls. Every inch of space within the catacombs is crammed with people, which over the centuries, have participated in the theatre of life here in Palermo; fathers and sons, mothers and aunts, the good and the bad. Rejoining Lucia and Greta, we peer into the cot of an infant girl called Rosalia Lombardo. Her golden hair is tied back with a large silk bow, and her porcelain skin appears so soft it looks like she is sleeping. I am struck by dozens of hollow eyes staring hauntingly in my direction. They act as a grisly reminder of how we humans live in the shadow of inevitable death. The obscurity of existence flashes through my mind. Thrust into the world, we grip on tightly to life aboard the beautiful blue and green planet we call home. Together we travel through time in a seething mass of love, laughter and hate. Hands overlapping, we cling to one another, the finality of our journeys, regardless of how unbearable we may be, no doubt the greatest challenge we face. Feeling mildly claustrophobic, I leave Chris and the girls transfixed by a finely dressed priest, whose mouth is gaping open in an apparent scream. I return to the deafening noise of the street outside. Inhaling a lungful of Palermo air, I savor the taste of blissful toxic reality.

Chris suggests we end our time together in Sicily gorging on seafood at a local restaurant close to Palermo harbour. Greta appears to have warmed to us both. It's a relief to be tolerated. Our journey to the ferry port is one of mixed emotions. Excited by the promise of what lies ahead, I feel a strong desire never to leave this island at the furthest point south of Italy's boot, in a land of personality, history, volcanoes, mega cuisine and sunshine. The Rover mounts the ferry ramp with a satisfying clang. It is a sound that echoes throughout the bowels of the vessel, announcing loudly and clearly that we will return.

Driving the Trans-Siberian
THE RAVEN BROTHERS

The Ultimate Road Trip Across Russia

Ever had the desire to jump in your car and keep driving, to wave goodbye to routine and commitment, to travel into the unknown with your arm out of the window hungry for adventure? Well, that is precisely what The Brothers decided to do whilst stacking boxes of frozen oven chips in a -30°C freezer. With a squeaky foot pump and an SAS Survival Guide, the travel writing duo fired up their rusty Ford Sierra and headed east.

After driving for six weeks and clocking up over 11,000 miles, quite literally living in the car, they miraculously arrived in the Far Eastern city of Vladivostok in Siberia on the Sea of Japan. What they had in fact done was to drive the entire length of the amazing new Amur Highway before it was finished, which crosses Russia and the notorious Zilov Gap in a 6,200 mile swath of cracked tarmac and potholes. Along the way our trusty heroes drink vodka with Chechen criminals, escape highway robbery, trade banana flavoured condoms with Russian cops, meet the eccentric and plain weird at truck stops in darkest Siberia, endure torturous road conditions and find themselves in a race to the finish with the Germans. Surviving the journey by the skin of their teeth, the brothers are forced to confront their worst fears in this toe-curling travel comedy of extreme road trip adventure.

Driving the Trans-Siberian is the second book in the 'Linger Series' travel trilogy.

Living the Linger
THE RAVEN BROTHERS

Freedom on the American Highway

Disillusioned with life in the big city, The Raven Brothers embark on a road trip from Seattle to Los Angeles through backcountry USA.

The sudden break up with Emily Willow finds Simon Raven, ex-amateur rock god and bored internet producer, on a Boeing 747 bound for Seattle. Led by his twin brother, Chris, who is more than happy to exchange a career in fashion photography for the open road, they embark on a buttock clenching journey of paranoia and self-doubt, as they traverse Interstate Highway 15 through backcountry America.

Along the way the hapless heroes bumble through bear infested wilderness, meet the eccentric and plain weird on the American freeway, escape a bullwhip wielding maniac in Montana and survive the evils of Las Vegas. Testing their friendship to the limit as they battle to reach their nirvana, which exists in the form of the bikini beaches of California, the brothers find inspiration on a journey that exposes the stark truth about work and relationships and which asks the question - what do you really want to do with your life?

Living the Linger is the first book in the 'Linger Series' travel trilogy.

Carnival Express
THE RAVEN BROTHERS

A South America Adventure

From bull's testicles in Buenos Aires to bums and boobs on the beaches of Brazil, The Raven Brothers embark on a new comedy adventure, as they attempt to traverse the Trans-oceanic highway from the Pacific to the Atlantic Coast of South America. Not always getting it right, the travel writing duo tango through the Argentinean vineyards, cycle to the Moon in the Atacama Desert, survive death roads in the Peruvian Andes and venture deep into the heart of the Amazon jungle, with only one mission in mind, to go in search of the real carnival!

Carnival Express is the third book in the 'Linger Series' travel trilogy.

Black Sea Circuit
THE RAVEN BROTHERS

An Adventure Through the Caucasus

The legends of Jason and the Argonauts, Noah's Ark and a tribe of fierce female warriors known as the Amazons all originate from the Black Sea. Gripped by curiosity, The Raven Brothers fire up their twenty year old Volvo that looks, "as rustic and weather-beaten as a Cold War tank" and embark on a quest to drive full circle around this ancient body of water at the birthplace of civilization.

In the shadow of rising tension in Ukraine, the brothers get up close and personal with the fascinating people who inhabit the six nations that surround these colourful shores. Living on the road like the nomadic horse bowmen who once ruled the steppe grasslands, they explore Crimea, the Caucasus region of southern Russia's "Wild West", the Georgian kingdom of Colchis, Turkey's Pontic coast, the megacity of Istanbul and complete their journey in Romania at the outfall of the mighty River Danube.

A career in overland adventure travel was launched when Simon and Chris coaxed a rusty Ford Sierra across Siberia from the UK to Vladivostok. Priding themselves in going it alone, the brothers have been noted by Lonely Planet for their talent to portray an "accurate view of what to expect".

Printed in Great Britain
by Amazon

50152605R00097